Mary Terese Donze

Teresa of Avila

PAULIST PRESS • *New York/Ramsey*

Library of Congress
Catalog Card Number: 81-85380

ISBN: 0-8091-2434-3

Published by Paulist Press,
545 Island Road, Ramsey, N.J. 07446

Printed and bound in the
United States of America

Acknowledgements

Somewhere there must be people who write books all on their own. I am not one of them. Others have helped me put together this biography of Saint Teresa.

I am particularly indebted to Benjamin R. Fulkerson, S.J., Professor Emeritus of Theology, St. Louis University, for checking the content of the story and offering clarifying comments; Walter Ong, S.J., international lecturer and author, for steering the manuscript through the final stages following on its acceptance by the editors; Etheldreda Heard, ASC, Ph.D., former Instructor in Education, St. Louis University, for laboring through the early draft of the manuscript and foreseeing its potential.

I also thank Helen Mandeville, Ph.D., Associate Professor of English at St. Louis University, for her critical reading of the earlier manuscript; Kathleen Jamieson, Ph.D., Professor of Communication Arts, University of Maryland, for help in revising parts of the story; Reverend Mother Mary Ann, Prioress of the Carmelite Monastery, Clayton, Missouri, for supplying details of the nuns' *horarium* and other relevant information; Carolyn Chapman, for countless suggestions and unfailing encouragement; Jan Nelson, for use of her travel literature on Spain; the librarians at St. Pius XII and St. Louis public libraries; all who expressed interest in the book's day by day development.

Thanks also to Donald Brophy, Managing Editor at Paulist Press, for his friendly attitude; Andrews and McMeel publishing house of Mission, Kansas, for permission to quote from *The Complete Works of St. Theresa*, translated and edited by E. Allison Peers.

My deepest gratitude is to the Saint herself for the inspiration she has been to me and for what I consider her guidance of the work from the pencil-paper phase to the final typing of the manuscript.

Lovingly dedicated
to the
Sacred Humanity of Christ

Prologue

This is the story of Teresa of Ávila, a sixteenth-century Spanish nun and mystic, and foundress of the Reform Carmelite Order.

The style of the text approaches that of fiction with its abundance of dialogue, but the conversation bits are relevant to the facts, and most of the talk lines are actual statements made at one time or other by the speaker. The italicized excerpts are directly from Teresa's *Autobiography.*

The men and women whose names appear in the story are likewise authentic persons, sixteenth-century people as real in their time as the people of today.

In writing the story of Teresa's life, I have taken the liberty to choose from several different interpretations put on Teresa's original Spanish statements. For example, in the incident concerning her cousin (Chapter 3), I assumed that it was Pedro and that the nature of his relationship with Teresa was as I have told it. In this I have followed Marcelle Auclair's lead in her book, *Teresa of Ávila.* I have also adopted Auclair's approach to the episode relating the friendship between Teresa and the cleric, Don Pedro Hernández, in Chapter 7.

Where I have made my own translations from the Spanish, I have allowed myself the freedom suggested by the nature of my manuscript.

1

"Rodrigo!"

Six-year-old Teresa, barefoot and trailing her long yellow skirt, stood in the doorway of the dark kitchen. She had crept down the broad stairs from her bedroom with an empty pillowcase in one hand and a pair of sandals in the other and was looking for her brother. Everyone else in the big house was asleep.

When Rodrigo did not answer, Teresa stepped into the kitchen. As soon as her eyes grew accustomed to the dark, she began to move quietly about.

It was early morning, August 1521. The sun would not rise for another hour, and the road that led out from the walled town of Ávila in Old Castile and on across the bridge toward Salamanca was quiet and deserted.

The big stone house at the far end of the road, where Teresa de Ahumada y Cepeda lived with her parents and a half dozen brothers and sisters, seemed quiet, too. The building's red-tiled roof and white walls were a soft gray in the half light of the early dawn. Behind the house in the patio, an ancient fountain splashed with rhythmic monotony into the circular stone basin beneath, and the air was heavy with the smell of dew on the flowers and plants. But inside the big house the usual morning peace had been disturbed and the day was getting off to a wrong start.

Less than two weeks ago news had reached Ávila of the infidel Turks attacking the island of Rhodes and beheading the Christian inhabitants. The grown-ups in the big house had discussed the report. They had spoken of the Christians as martyrs and praised their courage. Teresa had listened to the story.

"And the Christians went to heaven right away, didn't they, Mamá?"

Mamá Beatriz had agreed.

The idea of gaining unending happiness in exchange for a moment of pain caught Teresa's imagination. At last she determined to have her head cut off. Not in Spain. Her parents were too close. Maybe in Africa where the Moors lived.

Teresa confided her secret to her ten-year-old brother Rodrigo. After some hesitation, Rodrigo agreed to go with her. They would be martyrs together.

. . . even at so tender an age, I believe the Lord had given us sufficient courage for this . . .

Teresa heard a quiet step. Turning, she saw Rodrigo coming into the kitchen. He was wearing a dark red doublet with short matching breeches and a pair of soft leather shoes, but his sturdy brown legs were bare. A toy sword hung from his belt. When he saw Teresa, he took the worn felt hat that he carried and stuck it absently onto the back of his head, pushing his tousled curly hair up and away from his sleepy eyes.

"Come, Rodrigo. Hurry! Get us some bread."

Teresa had already dragged forward a high stool. Rodrigo pulled himself onto the stool. He opened the cupboard door and felt about the dark shelf until he found several large loaves.

"How many you want?"

"Two will be enough," said Teresa.

Rodrigo slid from the stool.

Teresa handed him the loaves. "Here." She opened the end of the small pillow cover she had carried from her bedroom and held it in front of him. "Put the bread in here."

Rodrigo dropped the loaves into the open pillow case. "We're really not stealing, are we, Teresita?"

Teresa shook her head vigorously. The short auburn curls that had clung matted to her head from sleep bobbed back and forth.

"Why, no. How can we be stealing? The bread belongs to our family, and we're family, aren't we?"

"Of course we are."

A short time later the two children were out of the house and walking briskly down the road. Rodrigo carried the sack with the two loaves of bread slung over his shoulder. Teresa marched beside him. Her long skirt, wet with dew from the grass, swished about her bare ankles and gathered the dust from the road into a narrow muddy border around the hem of her dress.

Here and there a few people moved about in the street. An old milk vendor with his groggy burro passed the children. Further along, a swineherd, driving a dozen grunting pigs out toward the open countryside, edged them off the road. But no one paid attention to the small travelers.

The children were outside the city gates and crossing the bridge over the Adaja River by the time the sun had fully risen. At the far end of the bridge, they stopped. The road divided here.

"I think Africa's this way, Rodrigo." Teresa pointed toward a range of low mountains forming a hazy, irregular blur along the horizon. Rodrigo turned with Teresa to the right and they followed the road along the river edge.

A short distance ahead of them a man was approaching on horseback. He came closer and drew up beside the children. "Ho! Ho!" The man lifted his hat and scratched his head as if to assure himself of what he was seeing. "What have we here? Where are we going?"

3

The children looked up. Teresa's face clouded. The man on the horse was Uncle Francisco who lived next to them in Ávila.

Francisco Álvarez de Cepeda was brother to Teresa's father. He was a married man with a family, but this morning, with the sunlight playing on his black wavy hair and the short, trimmed beard outlining his firm lower jaw, Francisco looked more the young, dashing cavalier than the father of a half dozen children, most of them older than Teresa.

Francisco looked at Rodrigo. "Where to?"

Rodrigo hesitated. He turned to Teresa, but she looked away and kept silent.

"Where are you going?" repeated Francisco.

Rodrigo squirmed. "To . . . to Africa!"

Francisco's eyebrows lifted. "Oh? To Africa? And does Mamá Beatriz know about this trip?"

Rodrigo took a deep breath and looked at Teresa. When she made no move to answer, Rodrigo raised his eyes to Uncle Francisco and shrugged his shoulders.

Francisco got down from his horse. For a while he stood looking at the young travelers.

"I don't know why you can't go to Africa if you plan to." Francisco stroked his beard thoughtfully. "But I think Mamá Beatriz should know about it. Suppose she decided to write to you. Where would she send the letter? Africa's frightfully big, I'm told."

Back in the house, fourteen-year-old María, Teresa's older sister, was the first to notice that something was not as it should be. She started down the broad stairway from her smaller sister's bedroom.

"Mamá, Teresita's not in her bed."

María was still talking when a younger brother, Hernando, ran into the house through the front hallway.

"Come! Come, Mamá!" He motioned his mother outside. "Uncle Francisco's here. He caught Teresita and Ro-

4

drigo running away." Hernando raced back through the hall and out the front door, leaving it open behind him.

Doña Beatriz, the children's mother, called to María. "Here, take the baby." She handed over the child she was holding in her arms. "Have the nurse put him back to bed. Whatever made him crawl out of his cot at this hour?"

"It's probably Teresita's fault, Mamá." María bounced the sleepy baby into the curve of her arm and went to find the nurse.

Doña Beatriz started for the door. She was tall and slender, and when she walked across the room with her easy step, her soft dove-gray dress fell faultlessly about her.

"Good morning!" came a hearty greeting from without. Through the open doorway Doña Beatriz saw her brother-in-law, Don Francisco de Cepeda, already inside the gate. He held Rodrigo by the hand. Teresa followed.

"Good morning, Doña Beatriz," Francisco called again when the children's mother appeared in the doorway. "Would you be interested in something I found down the road?"

Doña Beatriz looked disapprovingly at the small runaways. "Where have you two been?" She kept her voice low.

Rodrigo, still carrying the sack with the loaves over his shoulder, hung his head. "It's Teresita's fault, Mamá. She made me do it." He shuffled his feet uneasily.

Doña Beatriz glanced at Teresa standing behind. "Come here, *niña*."

Teresa stepped forward.

Beatriz studied the stubborn little face. "Teresita, go to your room until I send for you."

The small girl stood looking at her mother. Suddenly, without a word, Teresa threw her arms about Doña Beatriz's waist, burying a mop of curls against her mother's soft gown. The next minute she was running to her room.

Beatriz turned to Rodrigo. "Put your bundle away."

"Yes, Mamá." Rodrigo disappeared in a hurry.

5

"Where did you find the children, Francisco?"

"Half a league down the road." Francisco nodded in the direction. "Just beyond the bridge."

"What were they up to? Where were they going?"

Francisco laughed and slapped the dust from the sleeve of his green doublet.

"To Africa, mind you. To get their heads chopped off." Francisco related Teresa's plans.

Beatriz shook her head. "That little one!" Then she laughed.

2

At the age of six, Teresa, or Teresita as she was more often called, was one of seven children in the home of Don Alonso Sánchez de Cepeda and Doña Beatriz de Ahumada. María and an older boy were Alonso's children by a previous marriage. The others were Hernando, Rodrigo, Lorenzo, and an infant, Antonio. Later the family would be increased by three more boys and another girl, Juana.

Alonso de Cepeda was a fairly well-to-do man. He owned extensive estates, several houses, and a number of large herds of cattle. Alonso was also a religious man, fond of reading spiritual books and of saying his rosary.

> . . . *a man of great charity . . . He was strictly truthful: nobody ever heard him swear or speak evil. He was a man of the most rigid chastity.*

Alonso's piety did not make him stuffy. He knew how to enjoy life, and he wore fine clothes with absolute satisfaction. More than one head turned to look again after the trimly-bearded thirty-six-year-old Castilian with the high open forehead and warm friendly eyes, sitting tall in his saddle as he cantered along the streets of Ávila, the crimson plume in his black velvet beret bobbing with the horse's movements and his gold brocaded cloak, trimmed with sable and lined with cloth of gold, blowing in the wind.

Don Alonso delighted in this display of finery both for his own enjoyment and to please his girl-wife, Doña Beatriz.

Beatriz de Ahumada came of a noble family of Castile. She was fourteen when Alonso, almost twenty-five, married her. The magnificence of the wedding so overwhelmed the townsfolk that no one thought to gossip of the difference in age between the groom and the frail bride who leaned on his arm, tantalizingly beautiful in her silk, gold-trimmed gown, looking all the more lovely for being so young.

Beatriz was as prayerful as a nun, but she had a practical grasp of business—something Alonso lacked—and it was only after her death that Alonso realized how her shrewd management had been responsible for his continued prosperity.

Teresa was Doña Beatriz's third child. When Teresa was very young, her closest companion was her brother Rodrigo. He was four years older than Teresa, but she could be so bewitching and could coax so sweetly that time and again he found himself involved in one or other of her countless childish projects.

After their earlier attempt at martyrdom failed, Teresa persuaded him to join her in building a hermitage in the garden. They piled up stones for walls.

"Rodrigo," Teresa said one day. "I've been thinking."

"About what?"

"About how long *forever* is."

The thought of eternity was something Teresa had picked up from the stories Doña Beatriz had told the children about heaven and hell. The little girl kept puzzling with the idea, trying to get hold of its meaning.

"I know what it's like," volunteered Rodrigo. "It's like the fountain in the patio, where the water keeps coming and coming and never stops."

Teresa wrinkled her forehead. "Say it, Rodrigo."

"Say what?"

"Say *forever.*"

"*Forever,* Teresita. *Forever.*"

Through our frequent repetition of these words, it pleased the Lord that in my earliest years I should receive a lasting impression of the way of truth.

The mystery of a time without end never lost its hold on Teresa's imagination. It would later shape many of her decisions. For Rodrigo these early stirrings of the spirit were less enduring; his childhood awe was a touch-and-go experience. One day when the stone walls of their hermitage collapsed, Rodrigo's religious fervor cooled. Leaving Teresa among the ruins, he ran to play with the boys.

Teresa promptly gathered her girl cousins, Ana, Inés, and the others, daughters of Uncle Francisco from next door. She dragged out some of Doña Beatriz's old gowns and the girls played at being nuns.

. . . I used to love building convents and pretending that we were nuns and I think I wanted to be a nun, though not so much . . .

With napkins draped over their heads for coifs, they moved about the garden, eyes lowered, rosaries dangling from their hands. The cousins were older, most of them, but without any apologies or with-your-permission, Teresa took over the role of Mother Prioress, and it was she who led the prayers and gave the orders.

It was this irrepressible child who was both a worry and a delight to Doña Beatriz. María, the older daughter, was quiet and staid, more like her father. Teresa was lively, affectionate, often willful. But Beatriz did not favor Teresa. The young mother was devoted to all her children. She spent hours with them as they played around her in the patio where, with the baby in her arms, she reclined in a large chair. When the older children wore her out with their wild rompings, Beatriz would bring the younger ones into the house, give them over to the nurse, and retire to the quiet of her room. Teresa often followed her mother, and it was during these times together that Doña Beatriz spoke to her small daughter about Our Lady and the saints.

My mother . . . was a very virtuous woman . . .

Beatriz and Teresa did not always talk on religious topics. The young mother enjoyed the tales of chivalry then popular in Spain, and although she knew Alonso disapproved, Beatriz read these romances to the little girl who sat cross-legged on the huge cushions and listened with parted lips and wondering eyes.

. . . we were always trying to make time to read them . . . This annoyed my father so much that we had to be careful lest he should see us reading these books . . . I began to make a habit of it, and . . . unless I had a new book, I was never happy.

"Of course Teresa should learn about God and the saints, and I make sure she does," Doña Beatriz told Alonso one evening after the children were in bed and the two of them sat side by side and talked in the candlelight. "But it won't hurt her to hear these stories of brave heroes and heroines. She'll be encouraged to do great things, too."

Alonso frowned. More than once he had hinted to the woman at his side that the swashbuckling braggarts about whom she read were an immoral lot, bastards every one of them, and fathers of bastards. He turned to say this outright tonight, but checked himself when he saw his wife's face. In the glow of the candlelight Beatriz seemed even younger than she was, almost a child.

10

Was it a feeling of guilt that kept Alonso from speaking? He had deprived this woman of her girlhood, rushing her into the role of a mother when most girls her age were still free of responsibility. He was to blame for the repeated pregnancies that were breaking her health. Could he deny her the small pleasure she took in reading? There had been little enough romance in her life. Her marriage to him had been arranged. And with whom should she share her stories if not with this admiring little girl? María had no taste for reading; the boys were not interested; Alonso would not listen.

He changed the subject. He had bought a horse that morning, a good one. What did she think of the price? And had she heard that the olive groves in Andalucía weren't bearing well this season?

Beatriz had her own comments to make. María had been stung by a bee this afternoon while she was sitting on that bench under the acacia tree. The children got bee stings each year when the tree was in blossom. Should they, perhaps, think of removing the acacia? The boys had had a water fight around the fountain and knocked little Lorenzo against the stone basin. His howling had frightened her almost to death, and there was a lump on his head, but he seemed all right.

Alonso did not bring up the subject of his wife's reading again, and Doña Beatriz continued to share her novels with Teresa. At the same time Beatriz did not neglect Teresa's training. While she talked to her about heavenly and earthly heroism, she taught her to stitch, embroider, and use the spinning wheel. With her failing health, Beatriz felt that she would not live long, and before the time of separation came, she wanted to prepare Teresa in those skills the girl would need as a future help in the home and later.

Beatriz's premonitions of her own early death were not neurotic fancies. In November 1528, when only thirty-three, she died. Teresa was thirteen at the time.

Beatriz's death was Teresa's first experience of deep

personal loss. It left her desolate. At first she clung to María for comfort, but the two girls had little in common. Rodrigo, Teresa's childhood confidant, now seventeen, was interested in nothing but becoming a *conquistador* and crossing the sea to the strange, newly-discovered continent. Teresa found no companionship in him.

In her loneliness Teresa turned to the Mother of God. One afternoon in early December, a few weeks after her mother's death, she put on her long sheepskin cloak, drew a warm hood over her curls, and slipped away from the big house. She walked to the shrine of Our Lady of Charity at the hospice of St. Lazarus near the Gate of Adaja.

"Mary, you will be my mother now." Teresa looked up into the face of the Madonna. The outstretched arms of the Virgin seemed to reach toward Teresa in tenderness.

Though I did this in my simplicity, I believe it was of some avail to me; for whenever I have commended myself to this Sovereign Virgin I have been conscious of her aid . . .

After a while Teresa rose from her knees and walked away from the quiet shrine and back to the big house. She had been gone less than an hour, but as she pushed open the front door and went up the stairs to her room, she felt that a long time had passed and that suddenly she was no longer a child.

3

Two years had passed since Doña Beatriz's death. María, Alonso's oldest daughter, had taken over the management of the household. She was an efficient young woman, but caring for the large family was difficult. She sat now in the room overlooking the patio, sewing a white shirt for her father. The big house was quiet. Alonso had gone next door to see his brother on some business, and the boys were out playing. Suddenly the hallway door slammed.

"Is that you, Teresita?" called María.

"*Sí, sí,* María."

Teresa had come in from outside and was taking off her riding cloak. She hung it on a peg in the closet and started down the hall.

She was fifteen now, of average height, well built. Her dark eyes sparkled or softened with her mood, and her nose was straight and small. Her lips were full, her teeth white and even, and when she smiled she was excitingly attractive. She liked to brush her wavy chestnut hair back from her broad forehead and pile it high on her head, but this afternoon she had let it fall in soft curls, and she fluffed them back from her shoulders as she walked into the room where María sat sewing.

"Good afternoon, María." Teresa slipped off her gloves.

María looked up from her handwork and nodded.

Teresa smiled, then flushed slightly under María's continued gaze.

"Teresa, I don't think Papá would approve your and Pedro's going on those horseback rides . . . even though Pedro is our cousin . . . and even though you stay on our woodlot."

"But Cousin Elvira went along . . . and Lorenzo . . . for a while."

"All the same." María went on stitching. "Papá wouldn't approve. You and Pedro are together too often. People will begin to talk and Papá will be furious."

"But I don't see Pedro that often. Maybe twice a month. And is there anything wrong about my wanting to be with him? He's clever. He likes to ride"—Teresa gave the gloves in her hand a sharp twist—"and we like each other."

"That's evident." María looked up and smiled in spite of her concern.

Teresa laughed. "Don't worry, María." She bent and kissed her older sister's cheek. "I promise I'll never compromise my honor. And it really isn't that late, you know. The sun's still up. Where's Papá? I promised to play a game of chess with him this evening."

"He's next door with Uncle Francisco. Discussing the property, I think. Why don't you go to your room and brush your hair before supper?"

Don Alonso did not return for supper, and Cousin Diego came to say Teresa's father would be home later.

"I'll tell Papá you're waiting for him when he comes," said María when Teresa started for her room after the evening meal. María turned sharply as she spoke and boxed eleven-year-old Lorenzo who had been racing about the dining room all evening—taking advantage of Papá's absence—

14

and who at that minute had stuck out his leg and tripped young Antonio, sending him sprawling onto the floor.

An hour later Teresa, comfortable in the middle of a huge blue cushion, her head buried in a novel, heard a knock at her door. She hurriedly slipped the book under the cushion and picked up the box of chessmen and the playing board.

"Papá sent word you are not to wait for him," said María when Teresa opened the door. "He'll be later than he thought."

"*Gracias,* María. Good night."

"Good night, Teresita."

Teresa closed the door. How good María was. How responsibly she managed the family with their mother gone. At the thought of Doña Beatriz a shadow passed over Teresa's face, but it vanished almost at once, and Teresa dropped again to the comfort of her cushion and book.

During the weeks that followed, it was evident that María continued to worry about Teresa. At the same time she seemed hesitant to bring up the matter with their father.

But Don Alonso did not need anyone to tell him what was going on with his younger daughter. "Tell Teresita that when she goes to Mass Sunday she is not to use that perfume she had on today," Alonso told María one Friday when he intended to be gone over the weekend. "I don't like it. It's too . . . too . . . I don't like it."

I began to deck myself out and to try to attract others by my appearance, taking great trouble with my hands and hair, using perfumes and all the vanities I could get . . .

María was relieved to know that her father was noticing, but she bit her lips to hide her amusement.

"I'll tell her, Papá."

"Is Teresa beginning to use those foolish face creams already?"

15

María nodded.

Alonso snorted quietly. "Next it will be rouge, plucked eyebrows ..."

In January 1951, María married Don Martín Guzmán de Barrientos. The celebration was held at a small village about midway between Ávila and Castellanos de la Cañada, the future home of the young married couple. The festivities lasted several days, with dancing, singing, banqueting, and the usual amount of coquettish behavior on the part of the pretty *señoritas,* Teresa among them.

Alonso rejoiced in María's newly-found happiness, but he took sharp note of Teresa's lively conduct. Not that he thought she could do wrong. He trusted her too much.

So excessive was my father's love for me, and so complete was the deception which I practiced on him, that he could never believe all the ill of me that I deserved and thus I never fell into disgrace with him.

Four months after María's wedding, in May 1531, the Empress Isabel came to Ávila for the "investiture" of four-year-old Philip, later Philip II. It was to be a simple ceremony, nothing more than the change from the Prince's childish dress to his first royal breeches. Ávila had been chosen in accordance with the custom of yearly honoring a different city in the realm with some recognition. The town became the scene of jubilation. Its drab streets blazed with banners. Balconies and windows displayed rich tapestries. Games and tournaments became the order of the day, and the somber atmosphere of everyday life in this city of stones and granite towers gave way to the revelry of music, singing, and the clicking of castanets.

The day set for the investiture was July 26. Everyone prepared for the occasion. Next door, Uncle Francisco's sons, Pedro, Francisco, Diego, and Vincent, made ready to deck themselves in velvet doublets, starched ruffs, and silk-lined capes. For days the young gallants polished their swords.

Don Alonso's sons were making similar preparations, and Teresa and the girl cousins spent hours chatting about clothes, jewels, hair styles, and dance partners.

About a month before the festival day, María and Don Martín left Don Alonso's home, where they had been staying until their own home was ready, and moved to Castellanos de la Cañada.

María's departure gave Don Alonso the opportunity he was waiting for. Of late he had noticed a few things about Teresa and heard a word here and there that made him wonder. Now with María gone, he had sufficient reason for not permitting Teresa to participate in the coming festivities. She had no chaperon. Furthermore, he had other plans for her.

"Teresita," he said, calling her to his study about two weeks after María's departure. "I've made arrangements with the nuns at the Augustinian convent of Our Lady of Grace for them to accept you as a boarder."

Had Ávila's eighty-eight towers suddenly fallen about her, Teresa could not have been more surprised. She tried to look calm and indifferent, but her heart beat wildly, and a thousand thoughts crowded in upon her.

"María's gone," continued her father. "There's no one here to look after your training and education. The nuns are capable. They'll teach you the skills a young woman ought to know."

Alonso's words seemed to reach Teresa from a distance. When he stopped speaking, she heard a small voice asking, "When, Papá?"

Alonso picked up a letter from among some correspondence on his desk and let his eye sweep over the message. If he guessed Teresa's distress, he took care not to show it. "The arrangement is for the thirteenth. Today is . . . the sixth. Can you get ready in a week?"

A week! Everything inside Teresa rebelled. She wanted to shout. To say it was impossible to get ready in that time.

17

That it was impossible *ever* to get ready. Instead she answered quietly, "Yes, Papá."

She hurried back to her room. Her mind was a blur of questions. Why was she being sent from home? Had Papá heard about her and Pedro? Was this a punishment? How long would she be away?

She threw herself down onto one of the large floor cushions and stared blankly at the design in the carpet. A convent! Be buried in a home for nuns! How depressing! As for the festivity, she would no longer be part of it. The beautiful orange gown with its black velvet trim, the dainty slippers that fit her so well, her bracelets, the jeweled comb. What good would they do her now?

She got up and sat by the table near her bed, her chin cupped in her hands. Suddenly, bursting into tears, she put her head on the table and cried.

After a little she sat up abruptly, brushed away her tears, and took a piece of writing paper from a rosewood box on her table. For the next few minutes she wrote feverishly. A note for Pedro.

There was nothing in the note of which she need be ashamed, nothing anyone could not read. She simply told Pedro that she would be leaving, that she hoped she could see him once more to tell him goodbye. Nevertheless, she hesitated before sealing the letter. She knew she was laying herself open to criticism and suspicion should anyone find her out. No unmarried girl in Spain communicated with a young man without the knowledge of a *dueña* or chaperone.

It was this thought, that she was acting contrary to custom, that made her uneasy. She had already settled for herself that her feelings toward Pedro were not wrong, not something sinful. She had gone over the matter with herself dozens of times, even spoken to her confessor.

She sat now with the note in her hands and let her mind go back to how her attraction for Pedro had begun. It had been so simple. One of the cousins had told her that Pedro said he liked her. That had been enough. It would always be that way with her. Whenever she heard that someone liked her, she immediately responded with love.

Teresa recalled how at first she had been hesitant to allow herself the new and exciting emotion that stirred within her, but how later she had taken a few risks. Still, none of them had been any more serious than what she was planning now.

Eventually she sealed the message she had written. That evening she slipped it into the hands of a sympathetic servant.

. . . I found [the servants] quite ready to encourage me . . . Perhaps, if any one of them had given me good advice, I might have profited by it; but they were as much blinded by their own interests as I was by desire.

4

Teresa sat in her room at the convent of Our Lady of Grace and looked out onto the small enclosed garden with its clumps of mulberry trees and its narrow pathways. The afternoon was hot. The slight breeze that came through the open window was not enough to keep a few short curls from clinging to her damp forehead. Teresa brushed her hand upward and pushed them aside.

A month had gone by since her arrival at the convent. It was now mid-August. Teresa sat, holding a note in her hands and thinking of the past four weeks. She recalled the anger and frustration of those first days when she had none of the things she was accustomed to having—no mirrors, no jewelry, no complexion oils; and only the simplest of dresses. She remembered her resentment at not being able to attend the town festivity. But the anger, the frustration, the resentment had been as nothing compared to her loneliness.

Yet, here she sat, a month later, happy in this wretched house where there were only nuns and a few boarders like herself. Even the note from Pedro, slipped into her hands this noon by some intriguing go-between, had about it an element of the puerile; and, though in her loyalty to Pedro she

20

wanted to be angry with herself for feeling as she did about his attentions, Teresa crumpled the note and let it fall to the floor.

A sudden knock startled her. She rose quickly. "Come in, Doña María," she said to the tall nun who stood in the open doorway. "I've been waiting for you."

Teresa closed the door and they walked across the room to the window.

"Sit here, *Señora.*" Teresa offered Doña María the only chair in the room. Teresa settled herself at the nun's feet.

Doña María de Briceño was directress of the girls who boarded at Our Lady of Grace. Born a Castilian aristocrat, María had an innate refinement and natural charm. But it was her genuine affection for her charges that endeared the nun to the young ladies of rank who found themselves under her direction. Moreover, María was holy. She had a deep, personal love for Jesus in the Blessed Sacrament, and even before Teresa met her there was a growing legend that once, when María had been overlooked in the distribution of Holy Communion, two hands suddenly appeared bearing the Sacred Host to the devout nun.

Teresa had been in the convent less than a week when she confided to this gentle woman the bitterness and loneliness she felt. She even spoke to Doña María about Pedro, and María had understood.

The nun took the chair Teresa offered her. As she sat, her eyes went to the crumpled note on the floor. Teresa saw the glance and reached to pick up the paper. She smoothed it flat and handed it to Doña María.

"Read it, if you care to, *Señora.* It's from Pedro."

Teresa watched the nun's face as she read Pedro's avowal of friendship.

"You brought this with you?"

"No, *Señora.* I received it today. One of the nuns said it was given to her for me."

Doña María smiled, but she shook her head disapprovingly. "Against all regulations."

21

"I know."

"And, of course, you'll try to answer it through the same channels."

Teresa laughed. Both of them were aware of the change that had come over Teresa within the short time she had been at Our Lady of Grace.

> . . . I began to enjoy the good and holy conversation of this nun . . . This good companionship began to . . . bring back my thoughts to desires for eternal things . . .

Attractive clothes, cosmetics, useless chatter, and even Pedro were beginning to lose their hold on this girl in whose soul the grace of God was at work.

"I'm afraid of hell, Doña María," Teresa confided to the nun. "And the thought of eternity frightens me."

With her own clear perception of things spiritual, María was careful not to make light of the insights breaking over Teresa's soul.

"Perhaps you need to pray more, Teresa," suggested the prudent directress.

During the days that followed, Teresa was frequently in the chapel. One afternoon shortly before Christmas she was kneeling before the convent tabernacle. "My Lord," she prayed, "I don't want to get married; but I don't want to be a nun either. What do You want me to do?"

Teresa's decision not to be a nun had nothing to do with her stay at Our Lady of Grace. If anything, she had grown to like and admire the nuns and they had become very fond of her; yet Teresa could not see herself as one of them. At the same time the thought of eternity was never far from her mind, and often, when she sat alone in her room or went to pray before the Blessed Sacrament, the question kept coming to her: Wouldn't it be better to become a nun and live a life of penance and solitude to assure a speedy entrance into heaven after death? On the other hand, what if she became a nun and felt so embittered toward the life that she would end up with fuller punishment hereafter?

As for marriage, there was Pedro and her affection for him. Even while she thought of this possibility, her heart cried out for a love that lasted forever, something death could not touch. Marriage could not give her that.

She remained at Our Lady of Grace for eighteen months, but gradually her anxiety over her vocation began to undermine her health and she became ill.

The Reverend Mother sent word to Don Alonso. He came at once to take his daughter home. But even at home and with the best care that Don Alonso could provide, Teresa's recovery was slow. Her friends were impatient to have her join them again. Teresa, however, was glad that her weakness gave her an excuse to decline their invitations.

She found it more difficult to put off Pedro. His eagerness to renew their friendship, now that they were both older, could only mean that he was interested in marriage.

Teresa felt certain she would never marry Pedro even though she felt attracted to him and knew he loved her. She looked for ways of cutting short any visits from friends where Pedro was one of the group, and she never met him alone. At last, in spite of what it cost her in terms of hurting him, she refused to see Pedro any longer.

"Papá," she told her father one day, realizing it would be good if she left Ávila for a while, "María keeps begging me to stay with her for a time in Castellanos de la Cañada. She thinks the country air might make me well sooner."

Alonso was willing to try anything that might restore Teresa's health. He would miss her, for a new and deep understanding had grown between them since her return, but he made immediate arrangements for her to leave and got Rodrigo and Lorenzo to accompany her.

"Don't rush the trip," Alonso advised the boys. "Stop at Uncle Pedro's. It's on your way."

Pedro de Cepeda, Alonso's brother and like him a widower, lived at Hortigosa, a hamlet-size suburb of Manjaba-lago, a day's journey from Castellanos de la Cañada, the home of María. Pedro was a deeply religious man. Later he would become a monk. Now he divided his time between prayer and pious reading and the bringing up of his mother-less son.

As soon as Teresa met Pedro, she was won over by his piety and his evident affection for her. She stayed with him several days. The pious *hidalgo* let her browse through his li-brary, introducing her to the *Letters* of St. Jerome where she read a passage that was later to sustain her in a moment of indecision. Teresa and her brothers then moved on to Castel-lanos de la Cañada.

Once she was settled with her sister, Teresa began to feel stronger. She spent hours enjoying the open countryside and playing with her small nephew. She and María had long talks. They began to know each other better and to share confidences with an intimacy impossible when Teresa was younger.

5

The two-year visit at Castellanos de la Cañada did more than restore Teresa's health. It strengthened her resolution not to marry. María's life with her husband, Martín, was not unhappy, but Teresa recognized, in their example of married life, problems she felt unsuited to handle. She did not lack the courage to face life's difficulties, but she saw, in her confirmed resolution, a response to her prayer for guidance. She was glad now for the break she had made with Pedro.

When the time came for Teresa to return home, everyone in the big white house in Ávila was glad to have her back. Don Alonso particularly rejoiced to see his daughter once more under his roof.

Teresa was now twenty, a competent and charming young woman. How natural for Alonso to expect her to take over the home, care for her younger sister and brothers, and fill his wifeless days with her comforting presence. Lorenzo was sixteen and already beginning to be vain about his dress and looks. Antonio, fifteen, was a gentle, sensitive boy; there were two other boys, Pedro and Jerónimo, fourteen and thirteen. All of them adored their big sister. Then there were the little ones—Agustín, eight, a small terror, and Juana, seven. Rodrigo, of course, was now a man and busy making last-minute preparations for his adventure in the Indies. He had no need of Teresa.

For almost a year Alonso had his wish. Teresa was like another mother in the home. But it was a situation that could not last, and Teresa was the one who would change it. While she had stayed at María's, Teresa had decided that, in spite of her earlier resolve to the contrary, she was going to be a nun. It was only a matter of informing her father of her decision. The opportunity came one afternoon in late summer.

"You have something on your mind," Alonso said when Teresa came into his study where he sat behind a large desk working on accounts. He pushed the papers from him. "Are the children causing you trouble?"

Teresa shook her head. "No, Papá. I love them. But . . ."

"Sit down, Teresita." He motioned her to the large chair near his desk.

"Papá . . ." She needed to speak quickly before her resolution failed her. "Papá, I want your permission to become a nun."

Don Alonso started. He sat upright.

"You . . . you want what?"

"Your permission to be a nun, Papá."

Through the open window came the noise of a carriage passing the house. Alonso looked at Teresa. He moistened his lips several times. "Teresa, you are too beautiful to be a nun."

Teresa smiled and reached across the desk to lay her hand on his. "Papá, is anything too beautiful for God?"

Alonso got up from his chair. He walked to the window, gripping the flaps of his open jerkin, and stared out across the street and down toward the church of Santo Domingo de Silos. For a while he seemed to have forgotten Teresa's presence. From the patio on the far side of the house a child's laughter broke the stillness.

"You are not meant to be a nun, Teresa." Alonso spoke

without turning. "You belong in a family. Look how you've handled the children. You've held the household together . . ."

Teresa's eyes filled with tears. "Papá." She came up behind him and placed her hand on his arm. "Papá . . ."

It was too much for Alonso. He swung about and took her in his arms, holding her to his heart.

Teresa laid her head against his shoulder and cried softly. She had never known him so tender, and his reaction left her confused and uncertain. For a moment her resolution faltered. Was it right to cause a parent so much anguish? She struggled with the thought when suddenly there came to her mind those words from the *Letters* of St. Jerome, addressed to a youth also caught up in human attachments. "What are you doing beneath your father's roof, weak and cowardly soldier . . . even if your father himself lies across the threshold, step over your father's body. Here filial piety shows itself only by having no pity." Harsh words. But no more uncompromising than those other words, "He who loves father or mother more than Me is not worthy of Me."

Teresa looked up into her father's face. "Papá . . ." she said. But Alonso laid his fingers across her lips.

"No, Teresita." She could feel his whole body trembling. "My answer is *no.*"

"But, Papá, I must . . ."

"No. Not now. Later . . . Perhaps when I'm dead. But not now." He brushed Teresa aside and left the room.

In spite of her father's refusal to listen to her, Teresa continued to think about becoming a nun. Not at the Augustinian convent of Our Lady of Grace. The nuns there were admirable women, but some of their penitential and devotional practices seemed exaggerated to Teresa. She determined to enter the Carmelite convent of the Incarnation just outside the walls of Ávila.

The convent of the Incarnation had been founded in 1478, and had grown rapidly. By the time Teresa had decided to enter, there were about one hundred and twenty nuns living in the gray stone building north of Ávila. These women were heirs of the ancient Order of Carmel that held to a tradition claiming the holy prophet Elias as their founder. They looked back to a long succession of hermits who through the centuries had dwelt on the Mount of Carmel where once Elias headed a band of holy seers.

In the year 1200, Saint Albert, Patriarch of Jerusalem, bound these "Carmelite" hermits into monastic communities dedicated to the Mother of God and gave them a severely ascetic rule. However, after the Black Death of 1348 carried off many of the friars, some of the surviving monasteries adopted a less rigorous way of life. Custom eventually established this milder discipline. In 1432, Pope Eugenius IV officially approved the modified rule. The Carmelites who followed this rule became known as Carmelites of the Mitigated Rule. They were also referred to as Calced Carmelites—Carmelites "wearing shoes," the shoes being one of the concessions of the newer rule.

A few monasteries of the strict observance carried on, but their numbers decreased. In 1562, a year that would be significant in Teresa's life, the last monastery of Carmelites following the Primitive Rule was destroyed when the Turks invaded Cyprus.

The nuns at the Incarnation observed the Mitigated Rule. Their lives centered about prayer. They chanted the Divine Office, the so-called Hours. They rose at five in the morning, or six in winter, to begin their prayers. The day began with an hour of meditation or mental prayer. This was followed by the recitation together of the Hours of Prime, Terce, Sext, and None. Mass was at eight. At two in the afternoon the nuns sang or chanted Vespers. Compline, the Church's official night prayer, was prayed at five in winter and at six in summer. Later the nuns came together again for Matins and Lauds.

There was no rule of cloister at the Incarnation, and the nuns made full use of the liberty this allowed. If one of them wanted to visit a friend outside the convent, all she needed was the prioress' permission, which was easy to get especially when funds ran low in the convent and the food supply became depleted.

The nuns also spent much time with visitors in the parlors or "speak rooms." They wore a veil over their faces when speaking with anyone other than a relative, and barred partitions or grilles separated the nuns from their visitors, but the grilles did not prevent the exchange of small gifts.

Many of the nuns at the Incarnation were women with true religious vocations, but a fair number were women who for some reason could not find husbands or whose husbands had died and who felt that living in a nunnery afforded them more respect and status than otherwise would have been theirs.

Social distinctions, therefore, were clung to with jealous tenacity. The nuns coming from noble families retained their title of Doña. Wealth, likewise, made for differences among the nuns. Those from moneyed homes were able to furnish their bare cells (rooms) in comfortable, if not plush, style. The have-nots did with what little the convent could give them.

Many religious houses in Teresa's time depended, at least in part, on the charity of the townsfolk. The Incarnation was no exception. The nuns supplemented the alms of the faithful with the sale of stitched handwork and spun wool. However, since they were forbidden to set a price on their work and had to accept whatever the purchaser was pleased to offer, the nuns were not overwhelmed with revenue.

Among the Carmelites living at the Incarnation when Teresa began to think of entering was a young nun, a close friend of Teresa, Juana Suárez. Juana was to play a recurring, though minor, role in many of the later events in Teresa's life without, however, abandoning her position at the Incarnation.

Teresa did not choose the Incarnation simply to be with this friend. But neither did she choose it out of love for God.

Teresa wished this had been her reason. She lamented her "hardness of heart." She had watched some of the nuns at Our Lady of Grace weep at prayer, and she felt overwhelmed with shame that she could listen to a reading of the entire Passion of Christ without shedding a tear. Teresa's decision to be a nun was, therefore, less a matter of heart than of head. She weighed the risk to salvation outside the monastery, against the spiritual security that religious life seemed to offer, and she decided she had no real choice. She must be a nun.

> *I used to try to convince myself . . . [that] the trials and distresses of being a nun could not be greater than those of purgatory and . . . it would not be a great matter to spend my life as though I were in purgatory, if afterwards I were to go straight to heaven, which was what I desired.*

"What we need, Antonio, is a little determination." Teresa was talking to her brother who sat with her at the far end of the patio. The mid-September sun was warm, but the breeze was chilly and Teresa drew a light shawl closer about her shoulders.

Since Rodrigo's departure overseas, Antonio, though still a boy of sixteen, had become Teresa's closest companion. He had confided to her his intention of becoming a Dominican priest, and she had encouraged him. "But Papá will no sooner give in to your becoming a priest than he will to my becoming a nun. Still, when we know it's the only way we can save our souls, Antonio, we can't wait."

The big sister, who as a girl of six had convinced Rodrigo that having parents was the greatest obstacle to their chances of getting to heaven in a hurry, as a woman of twenty-one began persuading Antonio along the same lines.

A few more meetings in the patio and both of them were prepared to leave home without Don Alonso's permission. Antonio would present himself at the Dominican monastery of Santo Tomás in Ávila, and Teresa would go to the Carmelite convent of the Incarnation.

They set the date. Early one morning toward the end of October 1536, before anyone else in the big house was stirring, two shadowy forms, each carrying a small bag filled with a pitiful collection of belongings, descended the long stairway, unlocked the great wooden door that opened onto the street, and stepped into the gray of the chilly dawn.

When Antonio closed the heavy door behind them, Teresa suddenly stopped. Her hand went to her heart. "What's the matter? Did you forget something?" whispered Antonio.

"Nothing! Nothing!" How could she tell this generous boy at her side that she felt she could not go through with their plans.

. . . my distress was so great that I do not think it will be greater when I die . . . But the Lord gave me courage to fight against myself and so I carried out my intention.

6

Don Alonso sat in his study, but the work on the desk before him remained untouched. Less than an hour ago a message had come from *Señora* Doña Francisca del Águila, Prioress at the Incarnation convent outside the city. Did the *Señor* Cepeda know that his daughter Teresa had presented herself there that morning to receive the habit of the nuns?

The whole idea was incredible. Alonso had missed Teresa at breakfast, but he made nothing of it since she occasionally kept to her room for reasons he always learned later.

Alonso was puzzling now how to cope with this situation when notice came that Antonio, his "quiet" son, was at this moment begging to be received into the monastery of Santo Tomás.

Alonso groaned. "Holy Mother of God! What *is* this?" He threw a cloak about his shoulders and, donning a hat, called for his horse. He set off at once for the convent of the Incarnation. He would handle Teresa first. The boy would be easier to manage.

"Reverend Mother," Alonso said to the Prioress after he was admitted into the small parlor outside the grille. "I do *not* want my daughter a nun! I have not given my permission." His voice shook.

"*Sí, sí, Señor.* I understand." Doña Francisca was sympathetic. "I will call Teresa. She seems very happy, but we won't accept her without your approval."

The Prioress was not wrong in thinking Teresa happy. The instant the door of the Incarnation had closed behind her that morning, Teresa no longer felt any anguish. Her soul had been flooded with a supernatural joy that was never to leave her. Later she wrote of this day. "From the hour that I entered into this new life, I was filled with a joy that has never failed me."

Several minutes after the Prioress left Alonso, Teresa appeared outside the parlor grille. Her father rose when he saw her. Teresa ran to embrace him. "Papá!"

Alonso folded her in his arms. For a moment neither of them spoke. But the parental authority that Alonso meant to exercise broke down before the joy he saw on Teresa's face.

When he found a voice to speak, Alonso released Teresa from his arms. "I don't approve, Teresita." He spoke gruffly. "But I give my permission. I can see you won't be happy anywhere else." The trembling *hidalgo* took his thumb and traced a small cross on his daughter's forehead.

Teresa threw her arms about him once more. "*Gracias,* Papá." There were tears in her eyes.

"And now"—Alonso cleared his throat—"there's this matter of dowry. Maybe we should get that settled while I'm here." He sat.

"Yes, Papá. And the clothing."

"Clothing?"

"Well, I'll need something to wear until I'm a professed nun. After that the convent will take care of clothing me."

Don Alonso sat back and folded his arms. "Humph!" For a moment he regarded Teresa silently. Then he shook his head. "It seems to me, *niña,* that you've learned a great deal about this place in the few hours you've been here."

Teresa blushed a rosy pink and laughed merrily. "Papá, would a Cepeda take a step like this without first making some inquiries?"

Alonso grunted, but Teresa could tell he was pleased. Later she was amused when she learned from friends that he had gone about bragging that his Teresa was as practical as she was good and beautiful.

The dowry was agreed upon. Two hundred gold ducats each year or their equivalent in grain. Alonso would also send her bed linens and coverings, a mattress, pillows, a carpet. As for clothing, what did she want?

"I'll need material for two habits and for several veils. I have a sheepskin cloak at home. You could bring that along the next time you come. I should have some different shoes . . ."

Alonso got lost in the details. "Write me a list, Teresa."

Teresa received the Carmelite habit on November 2, 1536. She was radiantly happy. At last she was a novice.

"I can't understand where all this joy comes from," she wrote sometime later in a journal she kept for herself. "Everything here delights me. When I was sweeping the corridor this morning, I was amazed at the new happiness I experienced."

The joy was lasting, but it did not interfere with Teresa's previous determination to suffer in order to make up for her sins. She threw herself headlong into excessive penances.

She had been a novice a few months when someone was needed to fill the position of infirmarian. One of the nuns was suffering from an open abdominal ulcer.

. . . the nuns were afraid of it but for my own part I had only great envy of her patience. I begged God that He would send me any illness He pleased if only He would make me as patient as she.

Teresa saw in the sick nun an opportunity for making her penance practical.

34

"Reverend Mother," begged Teresa, "let me care for her."

Doña Francisca readily gave Teresa permission to nurse the ailing nun. But the constant stench in the invalid's room made it impossible for Teresa to keep food in her stomach. This, together with the long hours she spent in the infirmary and her nights of broken sleep, drained Teresa's health.

Each time Alonso came to the convent of the Incarnation to visit his daughter, he became more concerned about her condition. On November 3, 1537, a year after Teresa's Clothing Day, he came to be present at her Profession of Religious Vows. When he saw her that morning, Alonso was appalled. She had lost weight and the purple shadows under her eyes seemed deeper against the pallor of her face.

After the ceremony was over, Alonso drew her aside and, putting his arm about her shoulder, questioned her. "What's the matter, Teresa? What's wrong?"

Teresa shook her head. It was impossible to say what was wrong. "I don't know, Papá." Her illness was more than physical; her whole spiritual life was involved.

Whatever the cause, Teresa's health kept getting worse. She began to have extended fainting spells from which it was difficult to revive her. On more than one occasion word got around that Teresa de Ahumada was dead.

Finally Alonso took matters into his own hands. Early one morning he appeared at the gate of the convent of the Incarnation with a litter to carry Teresa back home. The Reverend Mother Francisca, worried about the young woman, was happy to permit Teresa to be taken someplace for a cure. She sent along Juana Suárez, Teresa's friend, to care for the sick nun.

When Alonso got Teresa back into his home, he dismissed the doctors who had been caring for her. He mistrusted their ministrations when he saw she was all the worse for their efforts. In desperation he resolved to take Teresa to a woman healer in Becedas, a small town not far from Castellanos de la Cañada where María lived.

7

In spite of the harsh weather, Don Alonso and his little company set out for Becedas immediately. Teresa traveled in a litter, tucked between warm blankets. Alongside, bundled against the cold winds and riding a mule, was Juana. Don Alonso led the group on a fine, black horse; several servants bumped along behind in a cart.

Becedas was fifteen leagues west of Ávila. The road the travelers followed passed through Hortigosa, the home of Uncle Pedro. Alonso had decided they would spend a few days with Pedro. From Hortigosa they would continue on to María's and then to Becedas.

Teresa was delighted with the stopover at Don Pedro's. She recalled with pleasure her earlier visit with this holy and learned man. Uncle Pedro was no less pleased to see Teresa. He embraced her warmly.

"*Bienvenida!* Welcome!"

With a glance Pedro took in Teresa's weakened condition; more especially he read in her eyes a new depth of spirit. When they were alone, he spoke of her spiritual life. Teresa was glad to confide in him.

"I don't know how to pray," she told him frankly. "I say the words, but I can't collect my thoughts."

They were sitting in Don Pedro's library at the time. Rising from his chair, Pedro reached for a thin volume on the shelf behind him.

"Read this." He handed Teresa Osuna's *Third Spiritual Alphabet*, an introduction to mental prayer.

For several moments neither of them spoke as Teresa paged through the book. When she looked up, her eyes shone.

"I can't believe it, Uncle Pedro. It's the way my heart has been telling me to pray, but I've been afraid."

On the morning they were to leave for Castellanos de la Cañada, Pedro found Teresa in the library copying passages from Osuna's book.

"What are you doing, Doña Teresa?"

"The impossible. Trying to write the parts I found helpful in this book, but they're endless."

"Don't bother." Pedro picked up the book and handed it to her. "My gift to you."

. . . I was delighted with the book and determined to follow that way of prayer with all my might.

Don Alonso returned to Ávila after he had accompanied Teresa to her sister María. It was still winter. The healer would not begin her treatment with Teresa until spring. It was April, therefore, when María, Juana, and Teresa left Castellanos de la Cañada for Becedas. They lodged in a house belonging to a relative of María's husband.

Becedas was a peaceful town, lying in the curve of a quiet river. Most of its small cottages clustered about the church, but here and there were farms with their open fields and orchards. If Teresa could have rested in these tranquil surroundings and enjoyed her newly-found treasure of prayer, she might have recovered her health without medical treatment. But the Providence that sometimes answers prayers in a strong fashion answered her petition for "the amount of suffering I need to save my soul" by permitting her to fall into the hands of this eccentric quack healer. At the same time this loving Providence watched over and protected her in another matter of greater significance to her soul.

Teresa was too ill to go to the church for her weekly confession. María asked the parish priest, Don Pedro Hernández, to come to the house. The curate, a man in his mid-forties, came with some reluctance.

María opened the door and greeted him. *"Buenos días, Padre."*

Don Hernández walked into the room. Teresa rose to meet him. The cleric was taken by surprise. Apparently he had expected to find a crotchety old woman. Instead, he saw before him this young nun who, in spite of illness, was strikingly beautiful.

Don Hernández bowed. He greeted her, and his dark, intense eyes searched her face. "Doña María tells me you are here to regain your health, *Señorita.*"

Teresa acknowledged Hernández's greeting and met his steady gaze with a warm, open smile. *"Sí,* Padre."

A half hour later the priest was walking down the path that led from the house and making his way back to the parish rectory. He would return each week and hear Teresa's confession.

Don Hernández was not a brilliant man, but Teresa found his conversation stimulating and his personality warm and engaging. Before long she began to anticipate his visits. One evening when she had gone to her room after having seen Hernández that day, she took out her journal. "I feel very fond of my Father confessor," she wrote. "I think he is fond of me, too." Her fondness for this priest was a natural result of her gratitude; that he was also fond of her made their relationship more pleasant.

At the same time Teresa was not ignorant of the scandalous rumors connecting her confessor's name with a certain woman in the village. Toward herself, however, Teresa had no reason to think he was other than honest.

Hernández continued his visits and occasionally he lingered to talk after hearing her confession. Did Teresa's holiness draw him? He had never before met a woman so good, so pure, so deeply in love with God. Or was he beginning to feel the natural attraction of her person? One afternoon he remained much longer than usual. That evening, alone in her room, Teresa sat before her open journal. She picked up her pen and wrote, "I think my confessor loves me in too human a way."

There was nothing wrong in his affection for me, but it ceased to be good because there was too much of it . . . it might have been purer.

Teresa did not, for all that, consider it necessary to discontinue meeting with Don Hernández nor to deny him her friendship. She felt that her intentions were blameless and that charity obliged her to be kind toward this man who was shunned and gossiped about and had no real friends.

Teresa had been in Becedas about two months. One afternoon in late June she had just completed a treatment by the woman healer and was seated in her room, reading and relaxing, when she heard a knock on the outer door. When no one answered the second knock, Teresa laid aside her book and went to the door. She was surprised to see Don Hernández.

"*Buenos días,* Padre."

Hernández seemed uneasy.

"Come in, Your Reverence."

He stepped into the room.

Teresa drew forward a chair. "Is something wrong?"

Without answering, and ignoring the chair, Hernández went to his knees. "Doña Teresa"—he had lowered his eyes and his hands were clasped before him—"I am not the man you take me to be. For seven years I have lived in sin because of a woman in the parish. Everyone in the village knows this. They talk behind my back, but because I am a priest, they do not openly reproach me."

Teresa was at a loss for an answer. She had accepted Hernández as a priest, a friend, but she felt certain that he knew she was aware of the village gossip. Why then this sudden open confession? At the same time Teresa felt shaken at hearing the scandal from the man's own lips. Seven years in sin! And saying Mass each day. A rush of compassion came over her.

I was sorry for him because I liked him very much . . .

Had Hernández foreseen this reaction of Teresa? Expected it? Hoped it would draw this beautiful woman closer to him? Was it of just such a situation that Teresa had made the entry into her journal, "His affection for me . . . might have been purer"?

Hernández rose from his knees. He stood facing Teresa. But if this was his moment of temptation, the strength and purity of Teresa's love for him saved him from his own weakness.

"Padre," she said, "God is full of mercy. Why don't you turn back to Him?"

Hernández said nothing, but his gaze faltered. Several minutes passed. Teresa spoke again. "Padre, come back to God."

Hernández opened his mouth to speak, but words failed to come. Instead, his face contorted in pain and his breath became labored. He seemed torn by conflicting forces.

Teresa bowed her head and prayed. Several minutes later she spoke to the wretched man. "Padre, what keeps you from turning to God if you will it?" She spoke gently.

The curate reached up and touched a chain about his neck. He drew it forth and Teresa saw a small amulet. She looked at the tiny brass idol and then at Don Hernández.

40

Was it possible the priest believed in witchcraft?

"Where did you get this, Padre?"

"*She* gave it to me, *Señorita.*" For the moment Don Hernández seemed little more than a frightened child. "I am her slave."

A sudden burst of anger shook Teresa. How the devil was deceiving this poor soul!

"Nonsense, Padre! Give it to me. Give it to me!"

The bewildered man fumbled with the chain, loosened the clasp, and handed the talisman to Teresa. Then he sighed deeply, like a man coming from a profound sleep, and gazed about him. He stared at Teresa as if seeing her for the first time. Suddenly he gave an anguished moan and sank again to his knees. The unhappy priest buried his face in his hands and sobbed convulsively. The spell was broken.

Teresa's physical energy was drained. She had been standing all the while. She sat now and she, too, cried.

Teresa continued to see Don Hernández each week, but he was no longer the same. He broke all communication with the woman in the village and his friendship with Teresa was completely in God.

A year to the day they met, the curate died, still penitent. Teresa, back in Ávila, heard of his death. Recalling this incident, she thanked God with tears for His mercy to the unfortunate priest and to her.

Years later, when Teresa had become a more mature woman, she was strong in condemning her conduct in this matter. "At that time," she said, referring to her days in Becedas, "I was so frivolous and blind that I considered it a virtue to be grateful and loyal to anyone who showed affection to me. Cursed be such loyalty when it threatens one's loyalty to God."

And yet, except for Teresa, Don Hernández may never have found his way back to God.

It seems that the Lord's will was that he should be saved by these means.

41

8

By the end of three months at Becedas Teresa was more ill than she had been before the treatments began. Her father hurried to bring her back to his home. She was unable to leave her bed and suffered intensely.

. . . sometimes I felt as if sharp teeth had hold of me, and so severe was the pain they caused that it was feared I was going mad.

Don Alonso lingered over her like a mother. Except when necessity called him away, he stayed by her side almost constantly.

"Papá," Teresa said to him one day in mid-August, the Feast of Our Lady's Assumption. "Get me a confessor. I want the Last Sacraments."

"Wait a little, Teresita." It would not do to let her think she was dying.

The day wore on. During the night Teresa sank into a coma.

"She's dead," said the priest, called to anoint her.

Don Alonso was inconsolable. He had let his beloved daughter die without the Last Sacraments!

The nuns at the Incarnation convent heard of Teresa's death and prepared a grave for her in the convent cemetery. Then they came with a cart to get her body for burial, but when they arrived at the house, Don Alonso refused to give up the body. He was like a man out of his wits, feeling Teresa's pulse, watching for a stir of breath, hoping for some indication that she was still alive.

For two days and nights Alonso did not leave Teresa's bedside. On the evening of the third day, worn out from lack of sleep, he asked his son, Lorenzo, now a young man of twenty, to watch during the night. Lorenzo sat by the table near Teresa's bed and moved the candle so that, while it gave him light to read, it lit up the ashen face on the pillow.

Around midnight Alonso, unable to sleep, got up and sat in his chair, fingering his rosary. Sniff! Sniff! Did he imagine it? Something was burning. He threw a robe around his shoulders and stepped into the hall. In the dimly-lit corridor he could see a thin cloud of smoke drifting from Teresa's room; on the wall opposite her open door, moving lights and shadows were making grotesque shapes.

"Fire! Fire!" Alonso ran into Teresa's room. The heavy curtains around her bed were in flames. Lorenzo, aroused from sleep by Alonso's cries, jumped to his feet. Together he and Alonso beat out the flames. In a matter of minutes the danger was over. The whole household had been aroused, but Teresa lay unmoving through it all.

On the evening of the fourth day the nuns came again from the Incarnation convent. They gathered about, determined on what had to be done.

Alonso ignored them. He sat by Teresa's bed, preparing for another night's vigil. Suddenly he started.

"She's alive! Teresita's alive!" Alonso pointed to Teresa. Her little finger was twitching.

Teresa had come out of the stupor, but her body was rigid except for the finger that was moving.

"A drink! Somebody get her a drink." Alonso looked at the nuns for a familiar face.

One of them ran for water.

"Try to drink this," said Juana Suárez, pressing the glass to Teresa's lips.

Teresa made an effort to swallow, but her tongue was swollen and her throat contracted. She choked on the water. However the crisis was over. She needed time to recover. By degrees Teresa regained full use of her speech, but her body remained paralyzed.

"Take me back to the convent, Papá," she pleaded after several weeks.

Alonso protested, but when Teresa continued to ask, he called for a litter and, along with Juana Suárez and several nuns who had come to accompany them, set out for the convent of the Incarnation.

In the convent infirmary Teresa needed constant attention. She was unable to move hand or foot. Her mind was clear, however, and in spite of her pain, her spirit was full of joy. Before long the infirmary became the common gathering place for the nuns. They scarcely allowed Teresa the solitude and time she needed for prayer. Teresa longed for the day when she would be well enough to return to the peace of her own cell.

Then one day, at Teresa's request, Juana and the infirmarian lifted her from her bed.

"I want to try walking."

The two nuns supported her, but Teresa's legs were too weak. She slumped to the floor. Juana and her companion bent to lift her. Teresa brushed them aside and crawled across the room.

"Thanks be to God!" breathed Juana as she and the infirmarian raised Teresa, bathed in perspiration, back onto her bed. It was Teresa's first full bodily movement in three years.

The doctors continued to watch over her slow progress. "You'll improve, Doña Teresa," they told her when she asked, "but you'll always be an invalid."

Teresa accepted their decision without comment. Later, when she was alone, she complained with childlike candor in prayer. "Lord, when I asked for suffering, I hadn't meant this much."

As if in answer to her complaint, Teresa felt inspired to pray for a cure.

> ... *when I found that* ... *earthly doctors had been unable to cure me, I resolved to seek a cure from heavenly doctors, for, though I bore my sickness with great joy, I nonetheless desired to be well again.*

Teresa turned to St. Joseph, confident that he would answer her petition. She was not prepared for the suddenness of his help.

One morning, shortly after begging the saint's intercession, she was sitting alone in the infirmary when she felt a strange power flow through her body. Placing one foot on the floor, then the other, she pulled herself upright, threw back her shoulders, and walked from the room.

She would never be a healthy woman. Until she was forty, she had difficulty keeping food in her stomach and she suffered from continual headaches, but the paralysis never returned.

9

"Someone for Sister Teresa in the parlor."

The portress passed the message along the corridor, and an obliging nun knocked on Teresa's door.

"Someone to see you, Doña Teresa."

These summons to the parlor were becoming routine. Teresa's relatives and friends, both men and women, were eager to see and speak with the young nun miraculously cured.

At first Teresa found these calls to the parlor burdensome. During her long illness she had looked forward to the day when she could return to her cell with its solitude and atmosphere of prayer. But the flush of health brought with it a new zest for life. Before many weeks Teresa found the parlor quite to her liking.

> I began, then, to indulge in one pastime after another, in one vanity after another and in one occasion of sin after another . . . [and] to lose the pleasure and joy which I had been deriving from virtuous things.

Teresa looked for reasons to excuse her conduct. She was unable to follow her brothers to the new continent to conquer and Christianize the Indians. But wasn't it possible, she asked herself, to evangelize here in the convent parlor? It took time, of course, and the hours spent in the speak room with some *hidalgo* or *señorita* meant less hours for conversation with Christ in prayer. Still, was that so great an evil if it meant winning a soul to God?

> *. . . I tried to lead [others] into the practice of prayer . . . I would show them how to make a meditation and help them and give them books . . . I was no longer serving the Lord according to my ability . . . yet [I tried] to be of profit to others.*

"Someone for Doña Teresa in the parlor."

Teresa gave a quick glance at her habit, flicked a bit of lint from her wide sleeve, and adjusted her veil. A minute later she stepped into the parlor.

"Papá!" She welcomed her father from behind the grille.

"*Querida mía!* My darling!"

Alonso had visited Teresa often since her return to health. These times together had been a joy to him. He and Teresa directed their conversation to God, and she helped him in his prayer life. Lately, however, Alonso had noticed a change in Teresa. God no longer seemed to hold first place in her life. Alonso intended to speak with her about it today.

"How are you, Papá?" Teresa broke in on his thoughts.

"*Bien,* Teresita. And your health?"

"Very good. Occasional headaches, but good."

Don Alonso sat silent for a while.

Teresa sensed there was something wrong. "What is it, Papá? Has anything happened to the boys?"

By now all but two of Teresa's brothers, Agustín and Antonio, had gone to the New World, and they, too, were preparing to leave. That October morning when Antonio had left the house with Teresa and gone to the Dominican monastery of Santo Tomás, he had been refused because of his age and lack of parental permission. Later he applied at a Jerónymite monastery but was compelled to leave because of poor health. Eventually, therefore, he decided to join his brothers in the Indies. Teresa was anxious about their safety.

"Teresa, nothing has happened to the boys. It's you. I'm concerned about you."

Teresa laughed lightheartedly. "Come, Papá. You worried long enough about me when I was ill. I'm all right."

Alonso looked at her. "You're different, Teresa. What is it?"

Teresa lowered her eyes from his honest gaze. She suddenly felt ashamed. This man whom she had led into higher levels of prayer had now surpassed her in his devotedness to God. Yet, she could be wrong. Maybe he wasn't thinking what she thought was on his mind.

"Different, Papá? How?"

Don Alonso did not answer at once. When he did, he questioned her. "How is your prayer life, Teresa?"

There was no use pretending. "Papá, if you mean mental prayer, I've given it up."

She caught the pained look in his eye.

"Don't worry, Papá," she added quickly. "I'll take it up again someday. It's only that I can't do it now with my headaches. I do well to get to chapel for the other prayers."

She knew she was not being sincere. She had just finished telling him how well she felt; now she was using her illness as an excuse. But Alonso believed her. His daughter would not lie to him. Nevertheless, he sighed and directed the conversation to news from her brothers. Shortly afterward he left.

Teresa went back to her room and closed the door. Her father's remarks had disturbed her. It would have been different had she been a careless nun, she told herself, but wasn't she considered one of the more devout at the Incarnation convent? If the other nuns could live so freely without appearing to violate their consciences why should she want to be different?

48

*. . . a great pity; for, when a convent follows standards
and allows recreations which belong to the world, and the
obligations of the nuns are so ill understood, the Lord has
perforce to call each of them individually . . .*

The Lord was calling Teresa, but she was not listening.
Her conscience, too, had taken her to task, upbraiding her
for a friendship she was carrying on with a frivolous *señorita.*

*I was once in the company of a certain person . . . when
the Lord was pleased to make me realize that these friendships were not good for me, and to warn me . . .*

Teresa tried to shake off the thought that the warning
might be from heaven. Couldn't the devil be trying to keep
her from helping this young woman? On the other hand, she
could not forget that repulsive, oversized toad that had
hopped wildly about the parlor floor the last time this undis-
ciplined *señorita* had visited her.

*I cannot imagine how such a reptile could have come . . .
in broad daylight . . . the incident made such an impression on me that I think it must have had a hidden meaning . . .*

However, the impression was not deep enough to make
her break off the friendship, and she explained away the toad
incident to her own satisfaction. Couldn't the portress have
been careless about closing the door to the garden?

*O greatness of God! With what care and compassion
Thou didst warn me in every way and how little did I
profit by Thy warnings!*

Shortly before Christmas 1543, Don Alonso suddenly
became seriously ill. Teresa got permission to care for him,
and she immediately left the Incarnation convent to be at his

49

side. Her presence with her father was a great consolation to him, but even her loving care could not save him. He died after a few days.

Teresa's heart had never been so broken, nor had she ever felt so much alone. Her brothers were gone, and while she and María had grown close to each other, there was not that same deep sharing in the spirit between them that Teresa had enjoyed with her father. As for Juana, Teresa's younger sister, she was but a girl of fifteen.

Teresa's conscience was also disturbed by the death of her father. The saintly dispositions with which Don Alonso had died made her think of her own unpreparedness for death. Immediately after the funeral, therefore, she approached the priest who had attended her father's deathbed, Father Vincent Barrón. She felt at ease with this learned Dominican priest and spoke at length with him, asking him to hear her confession and confiding to him her spiritual condition.

Barrón spoke kindly to the young nun. "Doña Teresa, what you need to do is go back to the practice of mental prayer and to receiving Holy Communion more frequently."

Teresa was grateful for the advice. She began once again to give herself to mental prayer. A few more years would pass before she would permit God's love to take over completely in her heart.

. . . the things of God gave me great pleasure, yet I was tied and bound to those of the world.

10

Teresa walked slowly down the dimly-lit corridor toward the convent oratory. It was early May 1553. The day had been pleasantly warm, but at sundown the air inside the convent of the Incarnation grew chilly, and Teresa gave a slight shiver. She tucked her hands under her woolen scapular.

Teresa was now thirty-eight. Ten years had passed since her father's death. During that time Antonio had been killed in battle at Iñaquito, in the New World; Hernando had become governor of a small Peruvian town; Lorenzo was growing rich in Quito; the other boys were carving careers in Peru and Chile. As for the girls, María was raising a family at Castellanos de la Cañada, and Juana, Teresa's younger sister, lived at Alba de Tormes, was married, and pregnant with her first child.

But Teresa was not thinking of her family as she opened the oratory door and stepped inside. The room was empty and dark except for the glow of one short taper that burned before some unfamiliar statue up near the front of the oratory.

Teresa was curious. She walked forward. Had one of

the nuns received a gift and placed it here until a more permanent place could be found? She stepped closer. By the flickering light Teresa saw that the statue was a bust of the Crucified Savior. Its realness took her by surprise. The thorns that crowned the head of the Christ might have been cut and twisted that day. The Sacred Face was bruised, swollen, discolored. From the uplifted eyes tears, blood, and sweat streamed down the pallid cheeks. In the shadowy stillness the Christ figure seemed alive.

Teresa felt a surge of pity. She made an involuntary move to touch the figure, but quickly drew back her hand. Suppose her fingers should become covered with blood!

Immediately her good sense rebuked her. How absurd to feel that way about a bit of plaster and glass. Nevertheless, a strange emotion had taken hold of her. She began to tremble. Suddenly she dropped to her knees before the statue and, without knowing why, burst into tears.

. . . begging Him to give me strength once for all so that I might not offend Him.

Afterward she could not remember how long she had knelt, but when she rose to leave, she knew something within her had changed, had broken down; something hard and obstructive had crumbled. In its place had risen again the clear, untarnished faith of her childhood. God. Eternity. These were what mattered. Nothing else.

"What's happened to Doña Teresa?" asked the nuns of each other in the days that followed.

"She had me excuse her to a young nobleman who waited an hour for her in the parlor."

"And did you notice her in chapel yesterday? I actually had to shake her to get her attention when Hours were over."

"Thanks be to God!" murmured an elderly nun, a distant relative of Teresa, who for a long time had been concerned about Teresa's conduct.

"Well, I only hope Doña Teresa isn't going to bore us all to death with her piety."

As the days went by Teresa became aware of a growing coolness toward her. Many of the nuns avoided her altogether. Gossip began to circulate among her friends outside the walls of the Incarnation convent, too. She who had always been happy when she found favor with others was now fast becoming unacceptable to those about her.

Teresa's new loneliness made her turn more often to God. One day as she knelt before the tabernacle, hurt by a cutting remark of one of the nuns, she heard Christ say to her in the depths of her soul, "Don't let their words cause you to fear, daughter. Serve Me."

The experience frightened her. It was unlike any prayer response she had known before. She had truly heard a Voice. Not with her ears; more surely than if with her ears. There had been that moment of happiness, but then she had feared. What if the devil were trying to deceive her?

Teresa looked about for someone in whom to confide. She finally spoke to Don Francisco de Salcedo, a holy gentleman who sometimes came to see her.

Salcedo, a friend of Teresa's Uncle Pedro, was pious and kind. He was also a learned theologian. When Teresa first met him, he was a married man. Later, at his wife's death, he prepared himself for the priesthood and was ordained in 1570.

Salcedo listened as Teresa told him of the Voice in her heart and of other favors Our Lord was beginning to bestow on her. The holy theologian was sympathetic, but he admitted to Teresa that he feared the responsibility her confidence put upon him. The Inquisition, a judicial body set up by the Holy Office in Rome to root out heresy, had been organized in Spain into a fanatical state court that was ready to ferret out and put to death anyone whose religious activities were suspect. Salcedo knew that a nun who professed herself to be hearing Voices or receiving Divine revelations would be ready grist for its mill.

Salcedo's fears were not unfounded. Ten years earlier the Inquisition had exposed as a fraud a certain nun, Magdalena de la Cruz, from Córdoba, who had deceived holy and learned clergy and laymen with her apparent sanctity. This infamous woman had posed as a mystic for forty years. She had inflicted wounds on her hands, feet, and side and had allowed them to be venerated as the Holy Stigmata. For over ten years Magdalena had made it appear as if her only source of sustenance were the Eucharist until, on investigation, food was found hidden in her cell. In 1544, under pressure from the Inquisition, the unhappy woman confessed that she had made a pact with the devil and that it was under his influence that she was caught up into feigned raptures and exercised powers that appeared supernatural.

Salcedo, therefore, was cautious. Was Teresa *positive* that Our Lord was speaking with her?

"Doña Teresa, I don't feel competent to judge on this matter on my own. Allow me to speak with Padre Daza."

Gaspar Daza was a zealous preacher, highly regarded by the citizens of Ávila. Energetic, with abrupt manners and a powerful voice, he nevertheless had the reputation of being a holy priest.

Don Francisco sought out Daza. He told the priest everything that Teresa had made known to him, her feeling of the continual presence of God, the Divine tenderness that was both a joy and a torment to her, the intoxication of love that lifted her out of herself.

Daza listened to Salcedo. "I can't understand," he commented. "You say that this woman tells you she is not a very perfect nun. Yet she hears the Lord's voice and is constantly aware of His presence. These favors are usually reserved for great servants of God, men and women of tried virtue."

The two worthy gentlemen shook their heads and pondered, while Teresa, full of fear, waited.

Salcedo finally brought her their united decision. "Doña Teresa, both Padre Daza and I think you would do well to discontinue mental prayer. As for these unusual happenings, consider them snares of the Evil One." Teresa felt distressed.

. . . I did not know what to do: I could only weep.

If what Salcedo said were true, how was she to proceed? How was she to handle these voices and visions when she did nothing to bring them on?

Fortunately Salcedo found a way to answer her. He had a good friend in the new Order of priests that was spreading over Europe, the Jesuits. Would Teresa speak to a Jesuit Father? Confess to him?

Teresa agreed, and the following week she bared her soul to Father Cetina.

Diego de Cetina was twenty-three years old. He was considered a man of indifferent ability within the Company or Society of Jesus. His Spanish superior once wrote in a secret report to Rome that Father Cetina was a fair preacher and could hear confessions but that he had limited potential. Nevertheless, this young, soft-spoken man listened quietly to what Teresa had to tell him, understood her supernatural phenomena, and advised her against giving up mental prayer, assuring her that she did not have to fear. "God is with you."

He left me comforted and strengthened.

In the spring of 1554, the Jesuit Francis Borgia came to Ávila. Borgia had been Duke of Gandía and favorite attendant on the beautiful Empress Isabel. At her death Borgia was so overcome by the sight of the Empress' disintegrating corpse that he vowed never again to serve a sovereign who could undergo such a change. His one thought thereafter was to follow Christ. A short time later Borgia's wife died, and he entered the Society of Jesus, the Jesuits.

Cetina asked Borgia to see Teresa. When rumor got around that this great Jesuit was going to interview Teresa, all Ávila was agog. Groups both in and outside the Incarnation convent waited to hear what this man of God would say about Don Alonso's daughter.

"The spirit of God is at work in Teresa de Ahumada," said Borgia.

I was greatly comforted . . .

The gossip ceased for a time.

11

Father Francis Borgia's approval of Teresa did not altogether assure Don Francisco de Salcedo. He and Padre Daza continued their investigation of Teresa's extraordinary experiences. They gathered a few other clerics to assist them, including Padre Gonzalo de Aranda, a priest in the vicinity of the convent of the Incarnation.

Aranda was a zealous man, but legalistic, narrow-minded, and unable to move beyond his own opinion. He joined himself to the group, however, and offered his suggestions.

"It's a ruse of the devil," Aranda concluded after he had been sufficiently informed as to what was going on. "Doña Teresa must trick the Evil One in his own act."

The group of men met and went to the Incarnation convent, where Teresa was called to the parlor. Gonzalo Aranda was the spokesman.

"Doña Teresa," he began, after being introduced to her, "the next time you think the Lord is before you, give him the fig."

Teresa was far from naive, but she stared at Aranda. "The fig, Padre? What's the fig?"

The men exchanged glances. The "fig" was a gesture of contempt of ancient and probably obscene origin that was thought to ward off the effects of witchcraft. It was made by inserting the thumb so that it protruded from between the first and second fingers.

Aranda cleared his throat. "It's a sign of contempt, Doña Teresa. Like this." Aranda demonstrated.

Salcedo moved uncomfortably in his chair, but Aranda was determined to see the matter through to the end.

"When you do this, Doña Teresa," he continued, "the demon will see that you have no use for him and he will leave you in peace."

Teresa made no comment on Aranda's ridiculous suggestion, but she looked from one to the other of the men sitting about. When she saw their serious faces, her first impulse was to laugh. Then she became indignant. The idea of giving the fig to the Divine Guest appalled her. But who was she to sit in judgment over men who had studied theology? Her humility overruled her good sense, and, bending her will to their authority, she made the foolish gesture when next the Gentle Vision showed Itself to her. At once she was full of apologies to the Divine Visitor.

"Do not worry, daughter," said the Voice in her heart. "You did right in obeying."

Teresa had no regular confessor at this time who might have given her support. Padre Cetina had been transferred to Salamanca.

"Let me introduce you to Padre Prádanos," offered Doña Guiomar de Ulloa, the rich young widow of Don Francisco Dávila, a woman for whom Teresa felt a great affection.

Teresa had met Doña Guiomar through the Jesuits at the church of San Gil, and the two women had immediately become close friends. From the first Teresa exerted a profound spiritual influence on the soul of this impressionable and ardent young woman who, though devout and charitable in her own way, led a life of almost scandalous extravagance. Little by little Guiomar began to moderate her way of living.

Before long the same tongues of Ávila that had gossiped over the reckless expenditures of Don Francisco's beautiful widow began to wag about the way in which the young woman was making her palace as austere as a convent. It was this woman who was suggesting Padre Prádanos as a new confessor to Teresa.

Prádanos was Doña Guiomar's own confessor. Meeting him would be a simple matter for Teresa since Guiomar's daughter, Antonia, was a boarder at the Incarnation convent and Teresa frequently escorted the young woman home.

Doña Guiomar did more than offer Teresa a confessor. She gave her free access to her palatial home, an offer Teresa could accept according to the rules at the Incarnation convent at that time. "You need the peace and quiet." Guiomar knew these were lacking at the convent, for either one or the other of the nuns was visiting Teresa in her room, or Teresa was being called to the parlor.

There was something else. For a time Teresa had been unable to resist the powerful forces that took over in her soul during prayer and reacted on her body. Several times the nuns had found her pale and rigid, her eyes closed, her pulse so faint they thought her dead. Teresa tried to keep secret what was taking place in her soul, and she pretended that each incident was the effect of a heart condition, but the nuns were not deceived.

Teresa spoke of these spiritual experiences to Padre Prádanos. He believed her and was able to offer her some guidance, but he was young and had limited knowledge in guiding souls. When he finally had to leave Ávila because of ill health, Teresa turned to Padre Baltasar Álvarez, also a Jesuit, for counsel.

Álvarez was twenty-four and had been ordained a year. His physical appearance marked him an ascetical man, with his thin lips and eyes that rarely softened. But under this stern and forbidding exterior was a heart sensitive and tender and dedicated to the service of God.

59

At first Teresa found Álvarez painfully exacting. A previous confessor had told her that, since her spiritual experiences had been confirmed as coming from God, there was no further need to speak of them or make an issue of them.

This seemed to me by no means bad advice, for whenever I used to speak about them to the confessor, I would be so distressed and feel so ashamed . . . for I thought my confessor would not believe me and would make fun of me.

Álvarez would have none of this reticence. If he was to direct her soul he wanted to be told all there was to tell.

This demand to know everything distressed Teresa. She would have found it easier to confess herself guilty of serious sin, had she been guilty, than to admit the Divine favors. She was not ungrateful for the loving intimacy with which God made Himself known to her, but how could she speak of it to someone else? Álvarez left her no alternative.

It was with genuine fear that she knelt before him in the confessional one day. "Padre, Our Lord is always standing by my side." She trembled as she spoke.

Álvarez affected a casual attitude. The last thing he wanted was a neurotic woman on his hands.

"Can you describe Him to me?" he asked.

"No, Padre."

"Why?"

"Because I can't see Him."

Álvarez stiffened. "How do you know it is Our Lord if you don't see Him?"

Alvarez's reaction increased Teresa's fears. Did he think she was lying? Would he refuse to listen to whatever else she had to say? But hadn't he commanded her to be frank with him? And now that she had told him this much, there was no point in holding back the rest.

"I can't explain how I know it, Padre, but I feel certain He is there."

Being completely ignorant that visions of this kind could occur, I was at first very much afraid, and did nothing but weep . . .

Teresa had found this disclosure difficult; she found other supernatural favors that followed even more embarrassing to put into words.

"I don't understand what has happened in my soul, Padre," Teresa told Álvarez on another occasion. "I was kneeling in prayer when an angel appeared to me with a golden shaft on the end of which was a burning flame. I think the angel was a Cherubim."

He was . . . very beautiful, his face so aflame that he appeared to be one of the highest types of angel who seem to be all afire.

"His rank doesn't matter, *Señora*. Go on."

Teresa felt her throat tighten. "He thrust the burning shaft into my heart." It was all she could say for the moment. Álvarez waited. "And then?"

"And then he drew out the shaft, but the flame stayed within my heart. I felt filled with a great love for God."

Álvarez made an effort to seem matter-of-fact. "But if it was a flame, Teresa, it must have burned. Didn't you feel the fire?"

"Oh, yes!" For a moment the memory of that blissful delight that had filled her at the time seemed to renew the rapture of the heavenly visitation. "I felt the fire. My whole soul seemed in an agony of pain. My body, too, felt the burning, but . . ."

"Well?"

"I never wanted the pain to stop. It filled me with such intense joy . . ." Teresa hesitated. What she was saying could not possibly make sense to anyone else. Pain a joy? But it was true.

. . . so excessive was the sweetness caused by this intense pain that one can never wish to lose it, nor will one's soul be content with anything less than God.

Yet how did one describe something that lay beyond words? While Álvarez was demanding these frank avowals from Teresa and causing her to suffer from his well-intentioned severity, he was at the same time fiercely supportive of her, defending her against men like Aranda, who saw the devil in her experiences, and fending off rumors and accusations that questioned Teresa's sanity.

Teresa found another champion in the Franciscan friar Fray Alcántara. Pedro de Alcántara was born in 1499, in the Spanish province of Estremadura. He entered the Franciscan Order when he was sixteen. The friar became one of the Order's reformers and was destined to be one of its canonized saints.

Pedro's personal life was starkly penitential. He seldom ate, perhaps once every three days, and never meat. By constant effort he had accustomed himself to sleeping but an hour or two each night. The holy friar never added to his clothing in winter or took from it in summer. His body, by Teresa's own description, looked like "tree roots." His prayer life was full of deep mystical experiences.

"You must meet him, Doña Teresa," said Guiomar, who hurried to the Incarnation convent when she heard that Fray Pedro was in the neighborhood and had lodged near her palace. "He's a saint!"

Teresa spent a week with Doña Guiomar. When she returned to the convent of the Incarnation, she had seen Pedro Alcántara and their meaning was the beginning of a lifelong friendship.

. . . he understood me . . . and told me not to be distressed but to praise God and be quite certain that it was the work of the Spirit . . . He left me greatly comforted . . .

Alcántara's approval of Teresa impressed the nuns at the Incarnation convent and made her more acceptable to them. Doña Guiomar took it upon herself to see that the curious and malicious of Ávila should also learn of Pedro's approval. By the end of 1560, seven years after Teresa had been "converted" by the sight of the statue of the Crucified Savior, the hubbub about her extraordinary prayer life began to subside. Holy men now openly approved her; her opponents had quieted down or forgiven her; Salcedo, Daza, and Aranda were completely won over.

The nuns at the Incarnation convent were less hostile, too. Teresa was once more allowed to resume a quiet existence among them.

12

Inés and Ana de Tapia, cousins of Teresa and Carmelites at the convent of the Incarnation, had come into Teresa's room and were stitching and talking with Teresa as she worked her spinning wheel. These two women were daughters of Teresa's Uncle Francisco and sisters to Pedro who had once counted so much in Teresa's affections. They had lived next door to Teresa in Ávila and had been her girlhood friends.

The afternoon was warm and the nuns' coifs fell limp about their faces, but the two sisters stitched industriously as they knelt on the floor and sat back on their heels.

Teresa's seventeen-year-old niece, María Cepeda de Ocampo, a boarder at the convent of the Incarnation, was in the room with the three nuns, settled comfortably on a floor cushion. She was a devout and intelligent young woman, but she had her full share of the Cepeda vanity, and she had carried with her to the Incarnation convent an enormous wardrobe. Today she was wearing a yellow taffeta dress, trimmed with ribbons and lace, and the long full skirt lay spread about her on the floor like some huge golden blossom. She was busy embroidering a cluster of pink-purple heather blooms on an oblong of soft black velvet.

María had only recently come to live at the convent. Usually she spent her days with the other boarders or with some of the younger nuns. Lately she had been seeking out her Aunt Teresa. Something in the way Teresa spoke of God attracted the young woman.

"Why don't all the nuns enjoy speaking of God and of holy things as you do, Doña Teresa?" María had just listened to Teresa relate the ancient glories of the Order of Carmel in so inspiring a manner that even Inés and Ana felt moved to devotion.

Teresa smiled. "It takes time to grow into some attitudes." She raised her voice about the whirr of her spinning wheel. "I used to like talking about clothes, dances, *hidalgos* . . ."

María nodded and smiled. "I remember your telling me how you almost died at Our Lady of Grace when you couldn't have these things."

Teresa looked at Ana and Inés. They were laughing. Both of them remembered Teresa's account of her experience as a boarder in the Augustinian convent.

"I was thinking, too . . ." Maria went on. She worked through the soft fabric as she spoke.

Inés stopped laughing. "We're waiting, María."

"I was just thinking how wonderful it would be if Doña Teresa and a few nuns who really love God got together and started a new convent. Maybe according to the Primitive Rule, the way it was before the Rule was made less strict."

Teresa continued her spinning, but she glanced quickly at Inés and Ana. Neither had raised her eyes.

"Would you join Doña Teresa and become a nun if she did?" asked Ana.

María laughed. "Don't rush me, *Señora*. But . . ."

"But what?" Ana prodded.

María sobered. "I'd give my inheritance to pay for the new convent."

"... a new convent ... according to the Primitive Rule."

Teresa sat in her room recalling María Ocampo's words from the day before. The idea was not new to Teresa. More than once she had allowed herself to dream of a quiet convent where God would be served in prayer and penitence, with no parlors, no visits outside the cloister. A place for women in love with God, not a refuge for *señoras* seeking security.

Teresa looked about the comfortable room she used as a private oratory and thought of her well-furnished bedroom with its fine view. "I wonder if I would have the courage to leave all this and start over?"

A week later Doña Guiomar visited the convent of the Incarnation. Teresa casually mentioned the conversation with María Ocampo and the Tapia sisters. "We talked about starting a new convent according to the Primitive Rule. Doña María offered to finance it."

"I'll help, too," said Guiomar.

Teresa laughed. *"Gracias!"*

"I'm serious, Doña Teresa. Aren't you?"

Teresa stopped laughing. "Not *that* serious—yet. We only just talked about it."

Teresa did not realize that a new direction was being given her life and that the choice of following it would not be left to her. The next time she received Holy Communion, she heard Christ say to her: "Daughter, do all in your power to found this new monastery. I will be honored by it. Tell your confessor I want it."

... the Lord gave me the most explicit commands to work for this aim with all my might ...

The command took Teresa by surprise. How could she, a woman, undertake such an assignment? Besides needing money, she would be involved in endless business concerns.

It humbled her, too, to think how difficult it would be to give up those two nice rooms at the Incarnation. Teresa delayed speaking with her confessor, but Our Lord was insistent.

> ... [He] appeared and spoke to me about it again and again ... that I dared not do otherwise than speak to my confessor ...

Álvarez did not question the command Teresa had received, but he puzzled about some practical difficulties connected with carrying it out.

"Where will you get the money, *Señora?*"

"I have some promised. Doña María Ocampo, my niece, offered me her inheritance. Of course, that would not be immediately available." The shadow of a frown passed over Teresa's face. "I hadn't thought this would happen so quickly."

Álvarez made no remark on her comment. If he felt sorry for her, he kept his thoughts to himself.

"No other money?" he asked.

"Doña Guiomar will help."

Money would be one problem. It might prove the least. What concerned Álvarez now was the reaction that would come once the matter was made public. He looked about for someone who could share the responsibility. "Doña Teresa, why don't you consult your Father Provincial? In the meantime, keep the matter secret."

At Teresa's request Doña Guiomar agreed to approach the elderly Carmelite Provincial, Padre Gregorio Fernández. The suggestion of a new convent coming from a young widow willing to help finance the project might carry more weight with the Superior than if it came from an unknown nun.

Guiomar went to see Fernández. She returned from the interview jubilant. The Provincial had given his approval.

The approbation of Fernández gave Teresa heart, but

Our Lord had warned her there would be difficulties. They began when the idea leaked out. All Ávila snapped to attention.

> *. . . there descended upon us a persecution so severe that it is impossible in a few words to describe it . . .*

"We don't need *another* convent," said the civil authorities, and the citizens agreed. "Ávila is filled with religious houses—Franciscans, Augustinians, Carmelites. They are enough drain on our charities."

The complaint was just. The 1570 census of Spain showed that of Philip II's 8,000,000 subjects, one out of every four adults was a cleric, a total of 912,000 monks, priests, or men in minor orders. The day-by-day support of these numerous ecclesiastics placed a staggering burden on the laity in the way of alms or benefice contributions. Besides the men, there were the nuns.

The religious Orders were concerned about Teresa's new convent, too. If the already meager alms of the faithful were divided to include another establishment, their own allotments would be cut.

Some of the clergy made no secret of their opposition. They ranted from their pulpits against "religious who depart from their monasteries on the excuse of founding new Orders."

Teresa sat through one such tirade. Her sister Juana was with her at the time. The young woman's cheeks burned with embarrassment at the evident reference to Teresa.

"How could you sit and let him insult you like that?" Juana asked when they left the church. "Had I thought you'd follow, I'd have walked out."

Teresa refused to speak against the preacher, but she was not indifferent to what had happened. She had been hurt by his remark. Intimacy with God does not dull one's sensibilities. Nor was she unconcerned about the offense that was being done to God.

I must reflect that the things are done to God before they are done to me; for when the blow reaches me, it has already been dealt to His Majesty by sin.

Teresa turned to Juana. "When people lose their tempers against me, I try to remember thoughts like these." She handed Juana a small bookmark from her prayerbook.

> Let nothing disturb you,
> Nothing cause you to fear.
> All things pass away.
> God remains ever the same.
> Patience gains everything.
> Whoever has God, needs nothing else.
> God alone is sufficient.

The nuns at the Incarnation convent were as upset as the townsfolk. "Who does Teresa de Ahumada think she is? She insults us, runs us down. So she wants to follow the Primitive Rule? Why doesn't she first show herself perfect in doing what the Mitigated Rule demands?"

The reaction from all quarters was so vehement that the Provincial, Fernández, withdrew his approval.

He said that the revenue was not assured, that in any case there would be too little of it, and that the plan was meeting with considerable opposition.

Teresa was disappointed and discouraged at Fernández's response. She turned to Álvarez, her confessor, for support. He too failed her. "Perhaps you should forget all about this, Doña Teresa. Someday you will look back and realize it was only a dream."

Teresa was stunned. A dream? How could he say that when he knew Our Lord wanted the project? What Álvarez did not tell her was that he had been pressured into this position by his rector, Padre Vásquez.

Padre Dionisio Vásquez was a cause of anguish not only to Teresa but also to his Jesuit confreres. He was a raspy, inflexible man. Later, when Claude Aquaviva became General of the Order, Vásquez and a group of malcontents, who were attempting to nationalize the Society of Jesus in Spain, were called to give an account of themselves, and some of them were expelled from the Jesuit ranks.

But now Vázquez had set Teresa's confessor against her; wherever she turned, she met with opposition and hostility. The few friends who stood by her were given the same treatment. On Christmas morning, when Doña Guiomar went to confession, the priest refused her absolution unless she promised to withdraw her aid from the project. (Guiomar looked for another confessor!)

What none of the opposition knew was that Teresa had already purchased a little house with some of Doña Guiomar's funds.

"What do I do now?" Teresa complained lovingly to Our Lord of the burden He had put on her.

"Remain quiet, daughter. Obey your confessor. All things will work out in the end. Wait."

Doña Guiomar, however, heard no voice telling her to wait. She and Teresa had a friend, Padre Pedro Ibáñez, a Dominican theologian at Santo Tomás. Sometime earlier the three of them had discussed Teresa's idea of founding a convent according to the Primitive Rule, and Ibáñez had pledged his support.

Guiomar went to this Dominican priest and, following his advice, wrote to Rome for authorization to finance the founding of a Carmelite convent where the nuns would observe the Primitive Rule and be under the jurisdiction of the Bishop of Ávila rather than under the Carmelite Provincial.

In the meantime a new rector was appointed for the Jesuit house in Ávila. He had heard of Teresa and approved her plans. Calling for Padre Álvarez, Teresa's confessor, he urged him to support Teresa. It was a happy moment for both Teresa and Álvarez. "But go about founding this house as quietly as possible," he told her.

Teresa agreed that this suggestion was prudent, but how did one set up a convent in secret?

The answer came in a circumstance no one could have foreseen. Teresa's younger sister, Juana, and Juana's husband, Don Juan de Ovalle, had decided to leave their home in Alba de Tormes and move to Ávila.

Juana had married Juan de Ovalle in 1553. The couple were poorly matched. Juana was a good, patient, home-loving woman. Juan, who had been a soldier under Emperor Charles V while the latter was fighting in Germany, was never able to settle down to life as a civilian. Furthermore, he was a naturally indolent fellow, and the family suffered from poverty as a consequence. But Juan liked his sister-in-law, Teresa, and he was ready to drop everything to please her when she called for his help. She was going to call for it now.

"God be praised!" exclaimed Teresa when she heard that the family was moving to Ávila. She immediately looked them up and told them her plan. Would they, for the present, move into the house she had purchased and pretend to set up housekeeping while she directed the renovation to make the place more like a convent?

At the Incarnation convent no one suspected anything out of the ordinary when Teresa asked permission to visit her sister Juana. Everyone thought she was helping the young woman settle in her new home.

The venture was a trying experience for Teresa. She was by nature frank and honest. Now she was obliged to carry on a wide-scale deception that made intimate communication between her and the other nuns impossible and set up a silent barrier between her and the Prioress whose position invited Teresa's confidence.

It was a lonely venture, too. Even those who loved Teresa and were in on the secret could not assume the responsibility. Teresa had been given the command. It was she who had to see it through, and she was never without the fear of being deceived. She felt the constant need of being reassured, especially by those guiding her soul.

> *...I did nothing without asking the opinion of learned men, lest in any way whatever I should act against obedience. As they saw what benefits ... were being conferred upon the whole Order, they told me I might do what I did, although it was being done in secret, and I was keeping it from my superior's knowledge. Had they told me that there was the slightest imperfection in this, I think I would have given up a thousand convents, let alone a single one.*

13

Don Arias Pardo de Saavedra of Toledo had been dead a year, but his young wife, Doña Luisa de Cerda, had never recovered from her loss. Luisa's family and friends feared for her health and sanity.

"If only you could speak with Doña Teresa de Ahumada, the Carmelite nun at Ávila," said a sympathetic friend.

Doña Luisa made inquiries about Teresa. The more she heard, the more persuaded she became. At last she called for her carriage and drove to see Gregorio Fernández, the Provincial at the Carmelite house in Ávila.

"Would Your Paternity consider giving Doña Teresa de Ahumada, the Carmelite nun here at Ávila, permission to live with me for a while?" Luisa sat across from the Provincial in the monastery parlor, the toe of her dainty slipper tapping nervously on the worn carpet as she spoke. "From what I hear about this nun, I have a feeling that her presence would help me."

Fernández's bushy eyebrows lifted, but his smile was paternal. He needed no persuasion. Wasn't this Teresa de Ahumada the nun who wanted to found a new convent? The one whose plans he had first approved and then felt obliged to reject? The woman had never approached him again. Perhaps she had given up the idea. Whatever the situation, it would be good to keep the nun distracted. And no doubt these two women would benefit from each other's presence.

Fernández's letter to Teresa, directing her to Toledo, reached her around Christmas 1561. Teresa guessed from its contents that her absence from Ávila would be more than a matter of weeks. She looked at the little house that was progressing nicely. "Am I to leave the renovation of Saint Joseph's and go to Toledo?" she asked Our Lord.

"Go. Have no fear. I will be with you."

Teresa set out for Toledo in early January. Her brother-in-law, Juan de Ovalle, and the faithful Juana Suárez accompanied her. For two days they headed their mules southwest across the bleak Castilian plains. They shivered in the sharp, icy winds. By evening of the third day they could distinguish Toledo in the distance. The city lay sprawled on its rocky height, silhouetted like a huge, purple shadow against the somber winter sky.

The following noon Teresa and her companions rode through the Bisagra Gate and into the town. This was Teresa's first sight of Toledo. She felt an immediate dislike for its raw red soil and brooding skies. Only the thought that she was coming here through obedience to her superior gave her any feeling of satisfaction as she and her two friends pressed their mules forward through the narrow, busy streets. On either side of them were rows of low, dark shops, humming with the activities of weavers, swordsmiths, candlemakers, and ironwrights. About two in the afternoon, tired and cold, they arrived at Doña Luisa's palace, urging their mules along the avenue of bare poplars leading up to the palace door.

Teresa's girlhood home had been moderately comfortable, but Doña Luisa's house with its elegant furniture, marble stairways, profusion of gold and silver plate was a treasure house. Everywhere Teresa placed a foot, her worn sandals sank deep into the thick colorful carpets. The candles that Doña Luisa burned in one month to light up her great dining hall would have supplied the nuns at the Incarnation convent for a year. In spite of all this affluence, Teresa saw at once that no one was happy here, least of all Doña Luisa. Not only was she still in a state of sorrow over her husband's death; she was overwhelmed with the responsibility of directing the activities of countless servants, maids, footmen, valets, pages. The young woman considered herself fortunate if the jealousies among her domestics did not break out into bloody feuds. Luisa's personal life was, likewise, hemmed in on all sides. Even in matters of dress and food she was bound by custom and convention.

Teresa was amazed to find the life of the rich so harassed. The romantic tales of her girlhood had led her to think otherwise. "Good Lord," she prayed after she had been in Toledo but a short time, "from what misery You have saved me by not making me a great lady!"

Teresa was a great lady in other ways, and Luisa found her interesting and lovable. They spent hours together. At times Teresa read aloud while Luisa sat and embroidered or simply listened and relaxed. At other times they conversed quietly, speaking of prayer and the things of God and exchanging confidences that drew them closer to each other. Even the time that Teresa spent alone in her room and at prayer was not lost for Luisa. Something of Teresa's presence filled the house.

It was while at Toledo and at the command of her confessor that Teresa began to write the story of her life. She did not write a simple autobiography, but an account of her soul's growth in union with God and of the Savior's manifestations of love to her. Teresa had mixed feelings about putting onto paper matters so personal and intimate, but once she gave herself over to doing it, she began to cover page after page with the praise of God's goodness to her and of His willingness to lead any soul along the path to holiness if only He found in it the necessary trust and abandonment.

Teresa had been with Doña Luisa only a few weeks

when word began to get around in the city that the Carmelite nun from Ávila was doing for Luisa what doctors, clergymen, friends had not been able to do. Everyone wanted to meet this remarkable nun. However, Doña Luisa kept them at a distance. Not every curious Toledan was given access to the palace.

"But you must meet my niece, Ana, the Princess of Éboli," said Luisa one day, presenting a twenty-one-year-old woman to Teresa. "Ana is the wife of Ruy Gómez, the King's personal advisor."

Ana de Mendoza de la Cerda had been married to Ruy Gómez, a Portuguese nobleman, a close friend and collaborator of Philip II. Their marriage had endured and their family of nine children been raised with some semblance of discipline only because of Ruy's patience and firmness. After Ruy's death, Ana began a scandalous relationship with King Philip's secretary, Antonio Pérez. The two were eventually implicated in a plot against the crown. Pérez escaped to Aragon, and when that fell, to Paris, London, and back again to Paris. Ana was placed under house arrest. She died in 1592, thirty years after meeting Teresa.

The young Princess was distractingly attractive. She stood before Teresa in a long scarlet skirt of brocaded silk studded with small pearls. Her close-fitting black bodice was trimmed with gold braid, and about her neck was gathered a high starched and fluted white ruff. Strands of miniature pearls interlaced the dark curls that were piled high on her head, and from a delicate gold chain in each ear two exquisite pearls hung down to her white neck ruff.

But it was Ana's face that held Teresa's attention. The Princess had lost an eye in duel play when she was still a girl, and she wore a black patch over the sightless eye. The dark patch accentuated the pallor of her face and drew attention to the other eye which was large and bright and might have been beautiful except that the long sweeping lashes did little to soften a look of smoldering arrogance.

Teresa acknowledged the introduction to this strange

woman, but her spirit felt oppressed by Ana's presence. Teresa could not guess at the time that this one-eyed woman would later be a cause of trouble to her.

Winter in Toledo warmed into spring. The white and rose blossoms of the almond trees bloomed and faded. The poplars that lined the avenue to Doña Luisa's palace grew rich with foliage. Outside the city, rows upon rows of olive trees burgeoned with new life, their hoary green leaves like a soft silver cloud hovering low over the groves.

During all this time Teresa received no word to return to Ávila and she continued to stay on at Doña Luisa's home. Her presence there had not only restored Luisa's health; it had made the young widow a sincerely religious woman. The household, too, had undergone a transformation. The servants worshiped Teresa. There was not one of them who had not at some time during Teresa's stay in the palace peeped through the keyhole of Teresa's door and seen the holy nun at prayer, her face alight with heavenly joy.

The Lord was pleased that, during the time I spent in that house, its inmates should come to render His Majesty better service . . .

Toward the end of May a stranger presented herself at Doña Luisa's door, asking for Teresa. She was dressed in a ragged Carmelite habit and called herself María de Jesús.

María was the daughter of a Granada lawyer. She was forty, seven years younger than Teresa. Two years earlier, feeling called to be a nun, she had applied at the Calced Carmelite convent in Granada and been accepted as a novice, but having come upon a copy of the Rule as given to the early Carmelites by St. Albert, she felt urged by an inner movement of grace to leave the Calced community and begin a convent according to the Primitive Rule such as Teresa hoped to do.

Along with several friends who shared her sentiments,

María had gone to Rome, walking barefoot all the way and leaving blood in her footsteps, to beg approval to open a convent according to the earlier Rule. On her return to Granada with the proper authorization, María had met with so much opposition that she had to give up the idea of opening a new convent in that city. It was then that she heard of Teresa and made the long trip to Toledo to see her.

Later in the summer, while passing through Madrid, María met Leonor de Mascareñas, the King's former governess, an energetic Portuguese spinster, pious and well-to-do, who offered María a house at Alcalá de Henares, a university town not far from Madrid where María made her foundation that same September.

"I advise you, Doña Teresa," said María as they talked together about their plans, "don't accept any endowments. The nuns should live from the work of their hands."

Teresa agreed that the nuns should work to support themselves, but until now she had also felt that the nuns should have sufficient security to relieve them from worrying about the necessities of life.

María stayed in Toledo for two weeks. By the time she left, Teresa had been won over to her ideal of poverty. Some time later, the unexpected visit of Padre Pedro Alcántara to Toledo and Teresa's few hours' conversation with him confirmed her intention to have her convent unendowed.

Teresa felt that the purpose of the Lord in bringing her to Toledo must have been that she get this spiritual advice. She wondered what more there was to hold her there. The signal that her work was finished in Toledo came in the form of a letter from the new Carmelite Provincial, Padre Ángel de Salazar, who had been elected during Teresa's absence. The letter ordered her back to the convent of the Incarnation. It was the end of June. Teresa had spent six months with Doña Luisa.

Teresa told her friends goodbye and returned to Ávila, taking with her the finished copy of her autobiography.

14

Teresa had written her autobiography at the command of her confessor, Padre García de Toledo, an eminent Dominican. In it she addressed herself to him, using the easy style of one who is speaking or writing to a friend, as indeed she was: "Your Reverence will know ..."; "Your Reverence may suppose ..."; "I should like to warn Your Reverence ..."

The book is a spiritual journal, and from time to time as Teresa writes and recalls the goodness of God, she breaks into words of spontaneous praise. "Blessed be Thou, O Lord ..." "O infinite goodness of my God!" "May I sing Your mercies forever since it has seemed good to You to manifest such great mercies to me."

In one section of the book Teresa tells De Toledo how she thought of her soul, of any soul, as a garden, a place where the flowers of virtue were cultivated and the weeds of sin and bad habits were uprooted. But for the flowers to grow and bloom, or even for the weeds to be loosened from the soil, it is necessary that the ground receive plenty of water. Prayer is that water.

Then, with the vividness of expression that was natural

to her, Teresa describes how the degrees of prayer can be compared to the ways by which the garden may be watered: by drawing water from a well with a bucket; by using a windlass to bring the water from the well by the turn of a crank; by a river or stream flowing through the garden or, best of all, by a refreshing rain.

It has seemed possible to me in this way to explain something about the four degrees of prayer to which the Lord in His goodness has occasionally brought my soul.

The first way of watering the garden is laborious. So with the first level of prayer. It is meditative, a work of the intellect, the understanding, where the results depend on one's own efforts and the prayer is not infused by God. The soul has need of recollecting the senses and focusing on the life and example of Christ.

For a time this attention of the mind on Christ will be easy and pleasant, and the soul will be filled with consolation. After a while, however, the understanding will become sluggish and the memory and imagination, dull.

It would be a mistake to think all is lost and try to force consolation at this time. Besides being useless, the effort may bring on depression and foster illusions. If the consolation disappears, it is because the soul no longer needs it, otherwise God would not have withdrawn it.

During this time of aridity the soul should remain peaceful, trusting that while the intellect is becoming inactive, the will is growing in power to love God more. Unless she is at fault through deliberate infidelity to grace, the soul should not begin to blame herself. Let her accept the cross of aridity lovingly and wait in silence.

I endured [these trials] for many years . . .

However, this is the time for courage and humility, for God is testing the soul's perseverance in prayer.

With each word that Teresa writes, she draws on her experience. She recalls her own mistakes and warns against them. The soul should not deceive herself into thinking that when all goes well in this prayer she is already a spiritual person and begin to take upon herself the guidance and correction of others. This is a temptation:

> . . . namely to desire that everyone should be extremely spiritual . . . Another temptation comes from the distress caused by the sins and failings which we see in others . . . and then we immediately try to set matters right.

On the other hand, when the going gets difficult, the soul should not be discouraged. God is aware of the way she is struggling to think of Him and love Him, and He asks nothing more than this.

If the soul perseveres in prayer, a time will come when she will feel drawn to put aside intellectual arguments, discussions, and clever reflections, and to rest in a simple, loving regard of God. This is the Prayer of Quiet, a level of prayer to which the soul cannot attain by her own efforts.

In this prayer there is less activity of the intellect and imagination, and the will is more at liberty to occupy itself with loving God. But the intellect and imagination are not bound or asleep as they will be in the higher levels of prayer. They may again intrude with their restless complexity onto the quiet of the will.

> What the soul has to do . . . is merely to go softly and make no noise. By noise, I mean going about with the understanding in search of many words and reflections . . .

The experience of the Divine Presence takes place in the "most intimate part of the soul." It is satisfying and delightful, but when the soul tries to explain or describe the satisfaction and delight, she lacks words.

Since the Prayer of Quiet is initiated in the soul by

81

God's action, it comes and goes at His pleasure. When it is present, let the soul rejoice in it; when it leaves, let her yearn for its return but make no effort to lay hands on it as if she had any rights to its possession. Instead, in times of aridity, the soul should be willing to go back to praying as she is able.

Above all, when the experience has passed, the soul should not allow herself to feel that the grace is gone forever, that it was an illusion, that to wish its return is a sign of pride. Rather, let her humbly acknowledge God's great goodness to her and realize that once He has granted her the Prayer of Quiet, it is a sign that He is calling her to even greater things.

Nor should the soul fear that she is being deceived by the devil. It will be sufficient to assure her that the prayer was from God if, after such an experience, she finds herself in great peace, if she practices virtue more sincerely, rises more quickly after each fall, is distrustful of herself while humbly trustful in God, and longs for solitude where she may again hope to find the Beloved.

Teresa pauses occasionally in her account to apologize to Padre De Toledo for the lack of coherence in what she is writing. It is because she has so little time. "I have my work to do," she reminds him—by this time she was back at St. Joseph's and revising parts of the manuscript—"and I can never write for a long time together. It would be easier if I could write when the thoughts come, but often I have to wait and write later."

After this digression Teresa picks up again, trusting De Toledo to remember where the thought was interrupted.

The third degree or level of prayer is a lesser form of the prayer of union still to come. At this level the faculties are so focused on God that they seem to have no activity of their own and are said to be asleep.

The soul is all but dead to the things of this world and intoxicated with such joy that she breaks forth in spontaneous and detached bursts of praise. The joy is so intense that it cannot be contained and causes pain to the soul, but a pain so excruciatingly delightful that she cries out, "More! More!"

This prayer, like all others, comes and goes. It is not a permanent state of the soul. The effects, however, are permanent and they assure the soul of the validity of her experience.

After having been raised to this degree of prayer, the soul will be aware of a great increase in the infused virtue of fortitude, together with a desire for martyrdom or a need for pain. She will also find herself no longer attracted to a desire for her own perfection. What God wants, His will, is her only interest. She abandons herself, body and soul, to Him that He may do with her as He pleases. If He chooses to accomplish great things through her, she performs them with no thought of self. It is He who is working in her.

In the former Prayer of Quiet the soul was so caught up in God as to have no desire but to remain in repose before the Divine Lover. In this prayer the excess of love in the soul spills over, as it were, and drives the soul to works of charity according to her vocation. It is not that she leaves God for the neighbor. She embraces the neighbor because she has too much of God to hold without sharing.

When Teresa begins to describe the fourth level of prayer, words fail her. "The fact is," she tells De Toledo, "when I began to write about this fourth level of prayer, it seemed as impossible for me to say what it was like as for me to speak Greek."

The way in which this that we call union comes, and the nature of it, I do not know how to explain.

However, one day after having experienced this highest degree of union with God after receiving Holy Communion, Teresa made an attempt to describe it.

This prayer is not something that ordinarily happens to

beginners. As a rule it comes only after the soul has practiced mental prayer over a long period of time. All the same, it is a pure gift, not a reward for the soul's perseverance. Some fervent souls never attain to this union in this life, and no one, to perfect union, which is reserved for heaven.

Neither can one predict the approach of the moment of union. Often it comes when the soul least expects it. Nor does it last for a long time. "I do not think I have ever experienced it for as long as half an hour." The entire prayer may last longer, but the periods of absolute suspension of the faculties is always of short duration, even though these periods may be repeated during the time of prayer.

The body is overtaken by weakness, deprived of movement. If the eyes are open, they are unable to see. But the strength that leaves the body seems to flow into the soul to support it in bearing the joy that accompanies union. Even this increase of strength in the soul is not sufficient to cope with the flow of delight, and the soul passes into a profound swoon, overcome by the unspeakable sweetness.

It is in this prayer of union that the soul dies wholly to self to live only in God and with His life. "It is not I that live; Christ lives in me." The intimacy of this union is so certain that the soul cannot do other than believe it is united with God, and the pain and sorrows of a lifetime would be as nothing in exchange for one moment of such bliss.

After this prayer has passed, the soul is left with a feeling of great tenderness, a desire to be "dissolved" and to be with Christ—not a death desire necessarily, but the desire to be lost in the Beloved.

A great influx of apostolic zeal fills the soul as a result of the prayer of union. She sees herself overwhelmed with gifts from God, freely given and endless in their Source, and she wants all to share in this great and constant flow of God's bounty. She becomes an apostle according to her way of life.

It was this manuscript that Teresa carried with her when she left Doña Luisa's house and returned to Ávila. The revisions that she later made in it were written during the odd moments she could snatch between her duties at the Incarnation convent and the supervision of the work on the new convent of St. Joseph.

15

The letter, or Brief, authorizing Doña Guiomar to found a Carmelite convent according to the Primitive Rule arrived from Rome the day Teresa returned to Ávila. Guiomar lost no time bringing the good news to Teresa. She found her at the Incarnation convent waiting for an excuse to get to St. Joseph's and continue supervising the renovations.

During Teresa's absence, Juana and her husband had returned to Alba de Tormes. However, the same week that Teresa returned from Toledo, Don Juan de Ovalle came riding into Ávila on business. Whether the summer's heat or Teresa's prayers were responsible, Juan felt so ill when he arrived in Ávila that he had to be helped from his horse and taken into the little home. Teresa was notified, and she came at once to look after him, bringing with her Juana Suárez.

"I can't thank Our Lord enough for the way He looks after this little house," Teresa told Juana one afternoon. Teresa had come into the small kitchen after having taken Don Juan a cool drink. She was carrying a bolt of frieze, a type of rough serge, which she spread on the table. "I'd been wondering how I'd get habits made for the four women who wish to enter here. With Juan sick, I can make the habits while I'm caring for him."

Juana helped cut and sew the material. They worked steadily. In two weeks four new habits, veils, and coifs were finished.

It was now the end of July. The workmen had put in the last dividing wall. Only one other matter needed settling before the convent could be opened. Teresa spoke of it to Doña Guiomar. "I haven't yet told the Bishop that I want the convent to be without any endowment."

The idea of establishing her convent without an endowment had become important to Teresa. As time went on and she set up more convents, she would have to give up this ideal of complete poverty and allow some convents to accept financial bequests to continue their existence. However, at this moment she had no thought of founding other convents as she approached the Bishop of Ávila with her request.

Bishop Don Álvaro de Mendoza had been prelate of Ávila since 1560. By 1562 he had not yet become acquainted with Teresa although he had heard of her. Eventually Álvaro was to become so impressed by reports of her sanctity that he requested they bury his body at death next to that of Madre Teresa. The Bishop died six years after Teresa and his body was buried according to his wishes. It remains in that place even today, but much of Teresa's preserved body is scattered in relics over all Christendom.

Doña Guiomar offered to take Teresa to see Don Álvaro. However, the Bishop was away at his country home, and Teresa had to be content with writing to him. She sent a second message to Padre Pedro Alcántara, asking him to plead her cause with the prelate.

Pedro Alcántara was desperately ill, but he climbed onto a mule and rode to the Bishop's summer house to speak for Teresa.

"What!" countered the Bishop when he understood what Teresa wanted. "Poor nuns! I refuse to consider the idea."

Alcántara went away without having changed the prelate's mind, but he got His Excellency's promise to see Teresa on his return to Ávila the following week.

A fortnight later the Bishop stood at the window in his episcopal palace, watching a Carmelite nun and her lady companion ride away in the lady's carriage. The Bishop smiled and shook his head. "Holy Mother of God! What a woman, that Teresa de Ahumada. When she sets her mind on something, who can refuse her?"

Álvaro had been completely captivated by Teresa's straightforward manner, her humility, and that indescribable blend of natural and supernatural charm that created in her a magnetic power. For a few minutes he stood silent, his thumbs locked in the broad belt of his soutane, his stubby fingers spread against his bulging paunch. Then he turned from the window and let his eyes move appraisingly over the luxuriously furnished study. "And she intends to live on the precarious assurance of alms!"

Ding! Ding! Ding!

The small bell at the convent of St. Joseph was ringing for the first time. It was early morning, August 24, 1562. The sleepy neighbors shook themselves and asked each other what was happening.

Inside the house Teresa was silently praising God for His goodness. In a few minutes the new convent would be officially established. His Excellency, Bishop Álvaro, had sent Padre Gaspar Daza to represent him and to celebrate the first Mass.

The small chapel was filled with friends. Teresa had welcomed Doña Guiomar, the convent's greatest benefactor, into the constricted space. Three nuns, Juana Suárez and the two Tapia sisters, had come secretly from the convent of the Incarnation. Don Juan de Ovalle, who with uncanny timing had recovered from his illness the day before, was there with Juana and their children. Teresa's two faithful helpers, Don Francisco de Salcedo and Don Gonzalo de Aranda, the "fig" priest, were also there, squeezed into the crowded quarters.

88

Serving Padre Gaspar at the altar was St. Joseph's new chaplain, Padre Julián de Ávila.

Padre Julián was a devout priest. As a youth he had run away from the Dominican College of Santo Tomás in Ávila where he was studying philosophy and theology. For two years he lived aimlessly in Andalucía. When he returned to Ávila, he met the priest Gaspar Daza. Under Daza's influence Julián resumed his studies and was ordained a priest in 1558.

Julián was thirty-five, of medium height, and inclined to be stout. He had a round, happy face and a short pointed black beard. The corners of his eyes crinkled with good humor. Julián later went with Teresa on most of her journeys, and some of the colorful reports of these travels come to us from Julián's letters that are full of a quick, cocky wit. Julián was kneeling now, in soutane and surplice, next to Padre Daza at the foot of the altar.

Everything was in readiness for the Mass. A spotless linen cloth covered the altar. On it were lighted candles and two small glass cruets, one with water, the other with wine. The four new habits, neatly folded, with the veils and coifs lying on top, were on a low bench next to the altar.

Daza blessed himself. *"In nomine Patris, et Filii, et Spiritus Sancti . . ."*

Peace filled the room.

The celebrant turned and faced the small congregation. At the same time four women, dressed in simple white gowns, each with a wreath of roses on her head and carrying a lighted candle, came slowly forward through the narrow aisle and knelt before Padre Gaspar.

"What is your desire?" he asked, reading from the Church's ritual for the consecration of virgins.

"The mercy of God, the poverty of the Order, and the society of the Sisters," the four responded.

"Thanks be to God!" exclaimed Teresa.

The small congregation echoed her exclamation.

One by one the four women stood before Padre Daza. "María de la Paz," he said, addressing the first, "you shall from now on be called María de la Cruz."

The custom of changing one's name when entering religious life has long been a practice in the Church. It is a symbolic gesture, as if the applicant were to say, with St. Paul, "I have died to the world that I may live unto Christ." The dropping of the name by which one has been known signifies this death. One's former identity is lost and the person becomes a new creature in Christ.

The novice offered her candle, and Padre Daza placed a habit, veil, and coif on the outspread hands of the young woman who had formerly been Doña Guiomar's little maidservant. In her pew the pious widow brushed a tear from her cheek.

"Antonia de Henao, you will be known as Antonia del Espíritu Santo," Daza said to the twenty-seven-year-old woman who next stood before him.

Teresa, kneeling near, reached out and squeezed Antonia's hand. "You have a saint praying for you," she whispered.

Antonia's eyes filled with tears. Her spiritual director, the holy Padre Pedro Alcántara, was too ill to attend her Clothing ceremonies, and Teresa's remark brought him to mind.

When María de Ávila came forward and spread her hands to receive the habit, Padre Daza lifted the religious garb from the bench and handed it to Padre Julián. The grateful priest, in turn, gave it to the novice, his own sister, and smiled when Daza gave her the new name, María de San José.

Last to receive the habit from Padre Daza was his own spiritual daughter, Úrsula de Revilla, a stout, ruddy-faced woman who had won Teresa's heart by her wholesome candor and unusual degree of common sense.

"My daughter," said Daza kindly, "receive the name

Úrsula de los Santos and know that even here God is permitting you to live among saints."

Teresa watched all this with a grateful heart. When the ceremonies were over, she thanked her friends and told them goodbye. Afterward she embraced her four spiritual daughters and welcomed them into their new religious family. Then, because she had slept only a few hours the night before, Teresa slipped away to her cell to get a few minutes' rest before the noon meal.

She had scarcely stretched out on her low cot when a host of doubts assailed her. Had she gone against obedience in establishing this convent without the Provincial's order? Would these four women be happy living such an austere life? Suppose they lacked food as happened at the Incarnation convent where sometimes the nuns had not enough to eat? Could she herself, with her uncertain health, sustain a life of continual penance?

She tried to relax, but it was impossible. She got up from her pallet and, leaving the room, went to the chapel. But even before the tabernacle she was unable to pray. She felt abandoned.

. . . my anguish was like a death agony.

She continued to kneel and wait for the Voice that had always comforted her. No Voice came, but by degrees a quiet peace returned to her soul.

Weeks later Teresa wrote of this experience: "I believe God allowed this conflict within me because I have never known what it is to be unhappy as a nun. I think He wanted me to know what a great favor He had granted me in giving me this unfailing happiness. I think, too, that He wanted to teach me that if ever I should meet someone who is unhappy as a nun, I should be compassionate and console her."

91

16

Teresa and her four novices were finishing their first meal together in the small room that served as a refectory at St. Joseph's. They had taken turns reading aloud from a pious book while they ate, refreshing their souls with thoughts of God while they nourished their bodies with food. As they rose to leave the table, someone knocked at the door. Teresa answered.

When she returned, she was calm, but her voice was unsteady. "I must leave you for a while. Doña Cimbrón has sent for me."

Doña María Cimbrón, a distant relative of Teresa, had been Sub-Prioress at the convent of the Incarnation in 1536, the year Teresa entered the convent. Now, in 1562, Doña María was Prioress over the one hundred and eighty nuns who made up the Carmelite community at the Incarnation convent. She was highly respected by the nuns, but it was her duty to maintain peace and a degree of order among a group of women not all of whom were minded to cooperate with her efforts. If then her black eyes sometimes flashed in indignation and grim lines appeared on a face already by nature lacking the softer elements, it was not necessarily that María

Cimbrón had an unsympathetic heart; rather, she was pressured by her position.

On the morning of August 24, when the new St. Joseph's convent opened, the word spread like a prairie fire across the city and beyond to the ears of Doña Cimbrón at the Incarnation convent. At once she sent for Teresa.

Teresa told her novices goodbye. "Sister Úrsula," she said to the oldest woman, "you will be Prioress here while I am absent."

The forty-one-year-old novice bowed her acceptance. Then all four women broke into tears and embraced Teresa. Each of them had known the difficulties connected with the opening of the new convent and the risk they had taken in joining Teresa. They guessed what might be awaiting her and wondered how their own lives would be affected.

"How long will you be gone, Madre?"

"As long as God permits. But be at peace."

"Father Provincial," said Doña Cimbrón to Reverend Ángel de Salazar, whom she had called to confront Teresa. "Here is the nun who has stirred up all Ávila." Doña Cimbrón's voice was brittle. "Everyone, myself included, thought that Teresa de Ahumada was helping settle her sister and brother-in-law in a new home in the city. As it turns out, *Señora* Teresa has opened the house as a convent."

The Provincial looked at Teresa. He was meeting her for the first time, but he knew from his predecessor, Gregorio Fernández, that she had asked to open a new convent. He had no idea that she had gone ahead with the project without permission.

Salazar realized he was in an unpleasant position. If he approved this nun and let the new convent remain, he would be accused of affirming a rival house of the Order and incur the wrath of the regularly established Carmelite houses. On the other hand, if the new foundation was manifestly a work of God, how could he withhold his sanction? It was an awkward and delicate situation.

"Gather the nuns into the oratory," said Salazar.

The Prioress pulled a cord near the door. The sound of a bell echoed through the convent halls.

Everyone at the Incarnation convent knew what was afoot. The nuns came, hurrying to take their places in the oratory. Teresa sat in her accustomed seat.

"Doña Teresa," said the Provincial, motioning Teresa forward to a position facing the crowd of nuns. "You know why you are here. What have you to say for yourself?"

Before Teresa could reply, dozens of voices called out.

"She has disgraced our Order!"

"She can't even keep the Mitigated Rule. How can she stand the austerities of the Primitive Rule?"

"She's a proud . . ."

"Enough!" bellowed Salazar, rising from his chair and bringing his hands together in a sharp, resounding slap.

When the room became quiet, the Provincial nodded to Teresa. She stepped forward and bowed to Salazar and the Prioress. Then she looked at the nuns.

For twenty-six years Teresa had lived with these women. She felt a warm affection for them, and in her need to be loved in return, she looked out expectantly over the group of Sisters.

"My dear *Señoras* . . ." Teresa started to speak. Her words were simple, sincere, contrite, like a child's admission of a misdemeanor.

> *I acknowledged my fault, as if I had acted very wrongly, and so in fact I must have appeared to have done to anyone who did not know all the reasons.*

Then she told them the reasons. When she stopped speaking, she dropped to her knees and, with eyes downcast, awaited a verdict. The room was quiet except for a few sobs from some of the nuns. The Provincial made a sign for the nuns to leave. The oratory emptied slowly.

Teresa was alone with the Provincial. There was no bitterness in her heart. The work she had undertaken was God's. If He meant to destroy it, it was for Him to do as He willed. She continued to kneel.

Salazar ordered her to rise and sit. Then he questioned her again about the new convent and listened to her repeat her story. In the end Teresa gained his admiration and support.

"But don't return to St. Joseph's immediately," he advised. "The town is in turmoil. When the uproar dies down, I'll authorize your return to your Sisters."

Teresa walked to her comfortable rooms down the hall. She was at peace, but her thoughts were with the women she had left at St. Joseph's.

The day after Teresa returned to the convent of the Incarnation, the Mayor of the city and his councillors called a conference to determine the fate of the new convent.

. . . they had all agreed that this new convent must on no account be sanctioned . . .

Representatives of the religious Orders were invited. The Mayor presented the charge, and all but two members—the Bishop's delegate and a Dominican theologian from Santo Tomás—agreed. However, when the meeting closed, no definite action had been settled upon.

The Mayor, therefore, decided to take the matter into his own hands. Early on the morning after the civic meeting, he came to the door of the small convent, bringing with him several constables. He knocked loudly and shouted his intention of breaking the door if the nuns refused him admittance.

The four women inside the house were far from being intimidated. Doña Úrsula shoved the table against the door. The other nuns ran for chairs, stools—anything they could find in the little house. Soon a barricade was set up inside the door.

The Mayor and constables heard the noise and guessed

what was happening. After some delay the magistrate dismissed the constables and returned to the City Hall.

The authorities wrangled for about six months. At last they grudgingly agreed to the presence of the new convent on the condition that Teresa find some regular source of income to supplement the alms.

Teresa was weary over the deliberations and eager to get back to St. Joseph's. She finally decided to give in to their terms. The night before she told the city fathers her decision, Pedro Alcántara, who had died a few weeks earlier, appeared to her.

"Madre," he warned her, "don't compromise. Once you give in to their wishes, you'll never be able to go back to your original plan."

Teresa saw in this vision a manifestation of God's will, and she held out against the magistrates. They finally dropped the matter and allowed the convent to remain—and as Teresa wanted it.

Teresa now asked and obtained the Carmelite Provincial's permission to return to St. Joseph's. She left the Incarnation convent at once, taking with her four nuns who had asked to belong to the new convent. Among the four was Ana de los Ángeles and a novice, Isabel de San Pablo, a cousin of Teresa.

17

Teresa was delighted to be back at St. Joseph's. She had a personal word of praise for each of her Sisters there, especially for Úrsula de los Santos who had held the small group together during her absence. She embraced the senior novice and said: "You are a prioress after my own heart, Sister."

The discipline in the house was still as Teresa would have wished it; the prayer, too, the meals, the silence, the charity. Teresa learned that the nuns had not suffered while she was away. Once the initial excitement had subsided, the townsfolk accepted the convent, began to love the nuns, and brought them alms without their need to beg.

The return to life under the Primitive Rule was easy for Teresa, but it was difficult for the four nuns she had brought with her. At the convent of the Incarnation their lives had been relatively comfortable. They had fasted and abstained from meat three days of the week, except during the penitential seasons of Lent and Advent when the abstinence was more strict. Their habits had been a fine cloth, and they wore shoes the year around. They had observed the rule of silence, at least to some degree; but no one in authority at the Incarnation convent frowned on the nuns' spending time in each other's rooms or speaking with relatives and friends in the parlors. It was easy, too, for them to get permission to spend days, weeks, or even longer periods of time with pious or devoted friends who desired their companionship.

Here at St. Joseph's, things would be different. As soon as the four nuns became a part of the new convent they were asked to fast every day of the week except Sunday for seven months of the year, never to eat meat, and to sleep on straw pallets instead of on mattresses. Their habits would be of heavy, coarse frieze. There would be no visits. Twice a day they would gather for an hour's recreation among themselves, but the remainder of the time would be spent in silence, prayer, and work.

Teresa knew that the change would not be easy for these four nuns, but she encouraged them with such sweetness and gentleness that soon they adapted to their new way of life and found a fresh joy in serving the Lord under the Primitive Rule.

One by one other women joined the St. Joseph convent. After Mass one morning Teresa called for Sister Isabel de San Pablo, the novice from the Incarnation convent, and said: "Prepare the small east room for a new postulant."

Isabel opened the window in the unused bedroom. She shook the straw pallet, covered it with a serge sheet, and slipped the pillow into a coarse linen cover. Giving the pillow a final pat, she picked up the pitcher from the small table in the corner of the room and went to fill it from the well behind the house. She walked quietly as the rule prescribed, but there was a suppressed excitement in her movements.

The expected postulant came shortly after the noon meal while the nuns were having their hour of recreation.

"Come in, and welcome to God's house." Teresa embraced the attractive, twenty-year-old *señorita* who stood at the door, asking admittance.

The other nuns came forward to greet her.

"Holy saints of God!" exclaimed Isabel de San Pablo. "María Ocampo! My cousin!"

Teresa had kept María's coming secret from Isabel to give the young novice the joy of the surprise. The two women threw their arms about each other. María's eyes filled with tears.

In choosing to come to St. Joseph's María had given up wealth, the freedom to do as she pleased with her life, and, not the least for her, the stimulating delight of beautiful clothes. In exchange she was being offered a way of life that demanded constant self-denial. But a year later, when she made her vows as Sister María Bautista, she was already a fervent nun, thanks to the grace of God.

Teresa loved this young woman who had once offered her inheritance for a "new convent . . . according to the Primitive Rule," and who was now bringing to St. Joseph's one thousand ducats to make good her promise. But Teresa tested the girl in many ways. Once, to see if María would obey even if the command were absurd, Teresa told her to plant a rotten cucumber. Without blinking an eye, the young woman took the cucumber. Before she left for the garden she turned to Teresa.

"Upright or flat?"

"Flat."

In April 1567, word reached Spain that the Father General of the Carmelites, Padre Giovanni Battista Rossi, was coming to visit all Carmelite convents and monasteries.

Rossi was an Italian, born in Ravenna in 1507. He was a man of medium height, heavy-set, with dark close-cropped hair, a rim of short, sparse beard from ear to ear, and eyes set widely apart. His natural urbanity easily won him friends, and he possessed qualities of leadership.

As a youth of seventeen Rossi had entered the Carmelite Order, and at twenty-nine he had graduated from the University of Padua. After graduation the young Carmelite went to Rome where he taught in the University of La Sapienza. He was well liked among the men of his Order, and in 1564, when the Carmelites held an election for a new

General Superior, Rossi, then fifty-seven, was chosen by an almost unanimous vote.

Rossi's headquarters were in Rome and he rarely left the Eternal City. But now he was on his way to Spain and eventually to Ávila. His coming was part of Pope Pius V's plan to have each Superior General visit the houses of his own Order and bring the practice of the religious into line with the recent decisions of the Council of Trent that had ended a year after the opening of St. Joseph's.

King Philip II of Spain—the same whose investiture into his first regal pants Teresa had once hoped to attend and then been disappointed and sent off to Our Lady of Grace convent—was eager to have Spain's religious Orders renewed. Philip, therefore, was happy to welcome Rossi to his kingdom.

Teresa felt uneasy about Rossi's coming. Would the General understand about her new convent? Would he believe that Our Lord had told her to establish St. Joseph's? Or would he disband her small community and send her back to the convent of the Incarnation?

When Rossi came to Ávila, he stayed at the episcopal palace of Bishop Álvaro de Mendoza, Teresa's friend. Mendoza told the General about Teresa and the convent she had founded. When the two men appeared at St. Joseph's the morning after the General's arrival, Rossi had only to meet Teresa to believe the good reports the Bishop had made regarding her.

Teresa immediately felt at ease in the presence of this kindly man.

I told him my story quite truthfully and simply, for whatever the consequences, I am always inclined to deal in that way with prelates, as they are in the place of God, and also with confessors, for otherwise I should not think my soul was safe.

Later that same day Teresa wrote of this visit in her journal. "The Carmelite General brought me much consolation. He told me I needn't fear being sent back to the Incarnation convent. He seemed very happy when he saw how we were living because he knew there was no need of a reform in our little convent."

Rossi had only one question to ask her. How could she justify placing herself and her nuns under the jurisdiction of the Bishop since she was still a member of the Incarnation convent and under the General's authority?

Teresa told him of the permission from Rome and showed him the official letter. Rossi looked at the form. He saw at once that it made no mention of the Bishop's authority. Actually it lacked permission for the Bishop's jurisdiction because its author in Rome thought that permission had been included in a prior letter.

Rossi called Teresa's attention to this omission. She brought out the earlier letter. He was right. She and her nuns were still subject to the Superior General. However, now that she was assured of Rossi's good will, Teresa saw no problem in acknowledging his authority.

A few days later she received a letter from him. In it he authorized her to found more convents according to the Primitive Rule, all patterned on St. Joseph's. The convents were to be confined to the province of Castile, and the Reform movement was to function within the original Order. In a flash Teresa saw her whole life changing. The peaceful years at St. Joseph's were over.

Several weeks later Teresa had another letter from Rossi. "Madre Teresa," he wrote in content, "you are hereby authorizied to found two monasteries of men similar to St. Joseph's." Two would be a beginning. The men could assume the future responsibility.

Teresa rejoiced that the work of the Reform was to include the friars. She folded the General's letter, put it aside, and set her mind for action. The action was to begin at once and it would cease only with her death.

18

The sun had just risen over Ávila. Its light flooded the towers and steeples of the city, and bells from every convent and church in town rang out the morning Angelus, that combination of triple bell tones that call the faithful to an age-old prayer honoring the angel's annunciation of Mary's Divine motherhood.

Julián de Ávila, the chaplain from St. Joseph's, guided his mule past some loose cobblestones in the street. "Good Lord! What a clatter!" He shook his head as if to rid his ears of the noise of the ringing bells. Julián was accompanying Teresa to Medina del Campo, a small town sixteen leagues north of Ávila, where she was going to establish a new convent in accordance with the Superior General's instruction. He sat on his mule with his faded black soutane drawn up about him on the saddle and his broad-rimmed hat pulled low on his forehead to keep the glaring sunlight from his eyes. As the bells continued to ring, he removed his hat and blessed himself. "The angel of the Lord . . ." The two servants, whose mules clomped heavily beside Julián's, muttered a prayerful response.

Behind Julián and the servants rumbled three covered

carts. In one Madre Teresa sat with María Bautista and Ana de los Ángeles. Four nuns from the Incarnation convent, including the two Tapia sisters, who were to be Prioress and Sub-Prioress of the new convent, were in the next cart. The last vehicle carried a few household utensils, some vestments, sacred vessels, and other articles for setting up a chapel in the new convent.

The small band set out on the road leading north. The weather was hot. The carts moved slowly along endless flat fields covered with sparse vegetation. Here and there flocks of sheep grazed quietly, nibbling at the scrubby growth. Overhead the cloudless sky blazed with metallic brilliance in the dry, clear air.

Several leagues outside Ávila they passed a group of merchants riding south on their way to Madrid. The merchants saluted Padre Julián and turned to stare at the strange covered carts.

Teresa's company traveled until dusk. But even on wheels, the nuns kept to their routine. Sitting under the canvas covers, they prayed their prayers together, kept their times of silence, and had their hours of recreation. Teresa had brought along a small hand bell, and she rang it for every change of activity.

By nightfall the group arrived at Arévalo where they planned to stay until the next morning. As they drew up before the inn, Padre Antonio, the Carmelite Prior from Medina, came out to meet them. Teresa had written to Antonio earlier, asking him to find her a house and get the necessary affirmation from the municipal and local church authorities.

Padre Antonio Heredia was Prior at St. Anne's at Medina, a monastery of Calced friars who followed the Mitigated Rule. He had been ordained at twenty-two and over a period of years had held offices of distinction within the Order. Antonio had worn the Carmelite habit and lived with the friars since he was ten, according to a custom of the times whereby children were sometimes permitted to live in the cloister with the monks or nuns. Teresa's eight-year-old niece would later do the same thing, running about the Seville convent in a habit cut to size.

Antonio's appearance at Arévalo surprised Teresa. He came forward to greet her. *"Bienvenida!"* He took her baggage and directed the group into the inn. His smile was warm and friendly.

After everyone had found accommodations for the night, Antonio drew Teresa aside. "Madre, what would you say if I suggested that you and your nuns return to Ávila tomorrow?"

"Return to Ávila? What are you talking about, Padre?" She gave him a puzzled look. "Didn't you write that you had a house for us?"

"I did, Madre. But it's next to an Augustinian monastery, and I learned last night that when the monks found out about your intention of establishing a convent, there was talk of a lawsuit if you took the house. I came at once to spare your making the trip for nothing."

Teresa laughed in spite of the annoyance she felt. "Padre Antonio, it will take more than a few monks to stop this work. Get your night's sleep. We'll make plans tomorrow."

The next morning Teresa arranged for the four nuns from the Incarnation convent to lodge at Arévalo until she should call for them later. Teresa and the others would go ahead. She planned to take over the house by night, before the sleeping Augustinians or anyone else would be aware of their presence.

It was close to midnight the following day when the tired travelers arrived at the entrance to Medina.

Antonio took over the lead. "Madre," he said, "there's no way we can do anything secretly with these noisy carts and mules."

"Very well," said Teresa. "We'll leave the carts and mules here." She stepped down from the cart onto the road. The other nuns followed and, along with the four men, the group stumbled through the dark, narrow streets, each making as little noise as possible, their arms loaded with pots, pans, brooms, altar linens, mats, and vestments.

After a half-hour walk through the dark, Padre Antonio stopped before a tumbledown building next to the Augustinian monastery. "Here we are!" he whispered triumphantly. He unlocked the door.

"Great Mother of God!" groaned Julián under his breath as he closed the door behind them and saw by the light of a candle the condition of the place. He opened his mouth to say more, but his words were lost in the noise of hooves pounding through the street outside.

Padre Antonio motioned the group to silence and, opening the door quietly, stepped back into the night. When he returned he was laughing, but it was evident that he was highly relieved.

"Madre Teresa, God is with us. Five minutes more in the street and we'd have been trampled under the feet of the bulls they're driving to the arena for tomorrow's games."

The travelers were exhausted from the day's journey, but there was no help for it—the place had to be cleaned. Teresa took hold of a broom. The two other nuns tucked up their long skirts, went down on their knees with pails of water that the men brought from an outside well, and began scrubbing the floor. Together then they set up a small table for an altar. The Prior Antonio helped Padre Julián and the servants carry away debris, put up the chapel drapes, and install the bell that they had brought with them.

By dawn the next morning, the feast of the Assumption, August 15, 1567, everything was in fair readiness. Padre Julián rang the bell and Prior Antonio, standing at the makeshift altar, blessed himself and began the Mass. The Medina convent was a fact.

The townsfolk gaped with wonder to find a religious house established in their town overnight, but they had no grievance against the group and gave them welcome. The Augustinians, faced with the evidence and realizing that Teresa had the approval of the local Ordinary, gave her no trouble.

Teresa soon saw that it would be impossible for them to remain in the house as it was. She looked about the town and found a generous merchant willing to rent part of his home to the nuns until they could repair their convent.

When the repairs on the house were finished, Teresa sent word to the four nuns at Arévalo, and eventually she and her six companions moved into the new convent.

Prior Antonio continued coming across the city from the Calced monastery of St. Anne's to visit Teresa or to say Mass for the nuns in this second convent of the Reform.

Teresa stopped him one day after Mass. "Padre, the Superior General has authorized me to open a house like St. Joseph's for men, but I don't know of any friar willing to take the risk."

"I will."

Teresa burst out laughing.

I took that for a joke and told him so . . .

Among the members of his own community of Calced Carmelites Padre Antonio had the reputation of being a devout religious. He was also well liked among the friars and was a possible choice for their next Provincial. But he was nearing sixty and there was a fussiness about his person that had not escaped Teresa. How could he adapt himself to the demands of the Primitive Rule?

Antonio continued to insist, and finally Teresa said: "Padre, give yourself a year of living the Primitive Rule in your own monastery. If after that you are still determined, you shall be my first friar."

One friar would not constitute a monastery. However, a few days later a young Carmelite priest who had just celebrated his First Mass at St. Anne's came to talk with Teresa. He introduced himself as Padre Juan de San Matías.

Padre Juan, or John of the Cross as he was later called, had entered the Carmelite Order of the Mitigated Observance in 1563. His father had died when he was seven. The family was desperately poor and the mother moved from place to place, trying to support her three sons by weaving. Poverty and privation were no new way of life for John when he became a friar. Indeed, his fervor for penance was so ardent that he was observing the Primitive Rule in a Calced monastery.

John was twenty-five when Teresa met him. He was short, less than five feet, and slightly built. His eyes were luminous with supernatural light and an aura of peace radiated from his presence.

Teresa looked at the diminutive friar and knew at once that he was the ideal man for her Reform monastery. His speech confirmed her judgment. A desire for God burned in his words, and Teresa sensed his thirst for penance and mortification. She could not hold off telling him about the Superior General's authorization for a monastery of men following the Primitive Rule. They talked for a long time.

"Madre Teresa, I'd be willing to offer myself for such a monastery, provided I'd not have to wait too long." John had already considered leaving the Calced and entering the Carthusians where the life was more austere.

"You have my promise, Padre," said Teresa as she knelt and bowed her head for the young Carmelite's blessing. "One year, no longer."

That evening during the recreation hour Teresa told her nuns about the Prior and the young priest. "I have a friar and a half," she said, laughing.

When I saw that I had two friars to make a beginning with, the thing seemed to me settled, although I was still not quite satisfied with the Prior.

19

Teresa stayed in Medina for two months after establishing the convent there. During that time she saw Inés prove herself a capable Prioress and the nuns leading a regular life, and thus she felt that there was no need for her to remain. She likewise saw the Lord indicating His will in a letter from Doña Luisa de la Cerda, the sick widow who had recovered her health when Teresa stayed with her in Toledo during the first half of 1562. Luisa was offering a house for another convent at Malagón, a day's journey south of Toledo.

Teresa was considering Luisa's request when Inés knocked at her door.

"Madre, Don Bernardino and Doña María de Mendoza, the brother and sister of the Bishop of Ávila, are here to see you."

Don Bernardino had come to offer Teresa a building for a convent at Valladolid. Teresa accepted his offer, but instead of going north to Valladolid, which was closer, she left Medina the next day to open the Malagón convent. She took Ana de los Ángeles with her as prioress of the new foundation.

The two stopped by St. Joseph's in Ávila. The community there was happy to have Teresa, but her stay was short. Don Bernardino and his sister María were in the city, planning to leave for Madrid and happy to take along Teresa and the nuns she had chosen for the Malagón convent.

Teresa set out with her benefactors toward the end of November. She chose a nun from St. Joseph's and five from the Incarnation convent to accompany her. The frosts had stripped the elms and sycamores, but the weather was not severe, and the trip was pleasant.

The nuns parted company with Don Bernardino and María at Madrid. Teresa and her companions stayed in the city a few days visiting Doña Leonor de Mascareñas, the pious spinster who had given a house in Alcalá de Henares to María de Jesús, the heroic nun who had once persuaded Teresa not to have endowed convents.

Teresa decided to take advantage of the nearness of Alcalá to visit María. The valiant María was a holy woman, but she lacked organizational ability. Teresa found her struggling to hold together her community, and at María's request she remained with her for two months. She gave María a copy of the Reform Constitution by which she was governing her own convents at Ávila and Medina. María accepted the Constitution but did not affiliate with Teresa's foundations. She and her community continued under the jurisdiction of the Archbishop of Toledo.

Teresa and her nuns moved on to Toledo, reaching the city on Shrove Tuesday. As they rode up the avenue of poplars that led to Doña Luisa's palace, the sun broke through a mass of leaden clouds that had darkened the day and its light burst over the city in a rush of bronze splendor. Teresa regarded the incident as a benediction on the new convent. It was not until Palm Sunday, April 11, 1568, however, that the house at Malagón could be established.

The ceremony was a festive occasion, different from the founding of St. Joseph's at Ávila or at Medina del Campo.

Malagón was a small, rustic settlement, a feudal community attached to one of Doña Luisa's old castles. Encouraged by Doña Luisa, all the townsfolk turned out to welcome the nuns.

That evening Teresa recorded the day's happenings in her journal: "The parishioners came from the town in procession. We went with them, walking in our white mantles, with veils over our faces, to the parish church where a sermon was preached. From the church the Blessed Sacrament was carried in solemn procession to our convent. The occasion was most consoling."

A month later Teresa was again on the road, leaving Malagón for Valladolid by way of Ávila. News had reached her that Don Bernardino had died, and Our Lord revealed to her that her benefactor would not be admitted to heaven until the first Mass was said in the Valladolid convent that Bernardino had sponsored. Teresa had once been shown a vision of hell. The sight of the torments endured by the damned had almost killed her. The thought that Don Bernardino might be suffering in purgatory urged her on.

She was delayed in Ávila by a visit from a relative, Rafael Mexía, who had heard she needed a building for friars. He offered her a farmhouse he owned in Duruelo, a hamlet about eight leagues from Ávila on the road to Valladolid.

"What a blessing of Providence," Teresa said to Padre Julián de Ávila and Sister Antonia del Espíritu Santo who were going with her to Valladolid. "We can stop on our way and look at the place."

The group left Ávila early on the morning of June 30, and should have arrived at Duruelo about noon the same day. As it turned out, they were given faulty directions, and the sun had already set when they saw the stone farmhouse up the road.

I always remember the fatigue of that long roundabout journey.

110

"Since it's late," said Teresa, "we can stay here overnight."

She had not counted on the impossible condition of the place. Apparently Rafael had not been near his property within the last year. The path to the door was overgrown with weeds and briars, and the dilapidated building, used for storing grain, was infested with vermin.

Sister Antonia, a stalwart woman accustomed to austerity, cringed at the sight. "Madre," she said to Teresa, "no matter how devoted one is to penance, he could not put up with this. Don't give it a second thought."

Teresa looked at the building and saw its possibilities. The large porch could be made into a chapel. The attic, with some few alterations, might be turned into a choir, and there was a large bedroom. However, she kept her thoughts to herself and directed Julián to find the village church where they spent the night.

The next afternoon when the group stopped by Medina, Teresa spoke to Prior Antonio and John of the Cross. "Padres, I have a home for you." She made no attempt to present the situation other than it was.

"We'll manage, Madre," said Antonio. He beamed as though he had been offered an estate. "I'm willing to live in a pigpen if necessary."

Teresa was surprised and pleased at this response from the elderly friar she had put on a year's probation. John of the Cross was no less eager. That night, tired as she was, Teresa got out her journal. "God has put into the heart of Padre Antonio a great deal more courage than I have," she wrote. The elderly Prior had gone up in her estimation.

Teresa stayed at Medina for a few weeks. She instructed John of the Cross on the application of the Primitive Rule before he set out for Duruelo. Antonio would follow later.

John's aptitude for the Reform was a source of unfailing joy to Teresa. She asked the nuns in the house at Medina to make him his first religious habit. When it was finished, Te-

111

resa passed it to him through the grille, and John insisted on putting it on immediately.

Padre Antonio, who had hoped to be the first friar clothed in the new vesture, accepted the reversal of roles with a good grace. Later Teresa made it up to Antonio by appointing him her first Reform Prior.

20

Teresa opened the Valladolid convent on August 15, 1568, the feast of Our Lady's Assumption. The site of the building was outside the city walls. The house had a large garden and a well-kept vineyard, but the nearby river created a health problem. Almost immediately the nuns fell ill with fever. Later María de Mendoza, Bernardino's sister, offered them another house inside the walls, and the nuns accepted the offer.

Teresa had felt from the start that this house by the river would never do. She had accepted it only to hasten the time for the first Mass for her benefactor. She wondered, as she prepared the altar for Our Lady's feast, if the Mass said here would be acceptable for her friend's soul since the house was only temporary.

As the liturgy began, Teresa prayed fervently for Don Bernardino. She pleaded with Our Lord that their benefactor be released from purgatory. When the time came for Holy Communion, the nuns walked up to receive Our Lord. Teresa raised her eyes and saw the figure of Don Bernardino standing beside the priest. Bernardino was dressed as Teresa had last seen him, but his face was suffused with light and he seemed radiant with joy. The happy man made a gesture of recognition and gratitude to Teresa and then vanished. Teresa's eyes filled with tears. That she was seeing a man who was dead and buried did not seem out of the ordinary to her; that God should be so good to this poor soul filled her with awe and thanksgiving.

Teresa remained in Valladolid until late February when she received a letter from a wealthy merchant, Martín Ramírez, in Toledo, requesting that she set up a convent in his city.

The roads from Valladolid going south were covered with ice or slush, and the countryside lay under a crust of snow. But weather conditions had never interfered with Teresa's plans. She set out with two nuns and the "fig" priest, Aranda, who happened to be in Valladolid at the time.

All winter Teresa had been eager to see how Padre Antonio and John of the Cross were doing at Duruelo. She knew that John had said the first Mass for the opening there on November 28, only three months after she had opened the convent at Valladolid. She had learned this from Antonio who visited her at Valladolid and reported on the progress of the repair job and told her about the furnishings he had picked up for the house.

"He came to Valladolid to talk with me," she wrote in her journal. "He was very happy and told me about the things he had gathered for their little house. It was a poor collection. What amused me was that he had five clocks. When I asked him why so many, he said he thought it important that they keep regular hours. He was more concerned about the clocks than about not having a bed."

Teresa determined to stop at Duruelo. She and her companions arrived early in the morning. As they started up the path to the small house, Teresa saw Padre Antonio sweeping the stone steps and she called to him. Antonio looked up when he heard the voice and, recognizing Teresa, dropped his broom and hurried to meet her.

Teresa threw up her hands in affected astonishment. "What is this, Padre? You sweeping? You, the Prior? Have you no regard for your dignity?"

Antonio laughed loudly. "A plague on the day I ever thought I had any dignity." He led them into the house. The friars had repaired and cleaned the old stone farmhouse. The floors and walls were spotless. Even more notable than the absence of dirt was the evidence of poverty and simplicity.

. . . when I saw that little house, which so recently it had been impossible to live in, filled with such spirituality that, wherever I looked, I seemed to find cause for edification . . . I could not give Our Lord sufficient thanks, so great was my inward joy, for I thought I had seen a beginning made to the great profit of our Order and the service of Our Lord.

"I can't forget the little wooden cross I saw above the holy water basin," Teresa jotted down in her journal that evening. "The picture of Christ that was pasted on it was of paper, but it inspired everyone with more devotion than if it had been an expensive carving."

Teresa and her companions reached Toledo in early March. The olive groves outside the city were still without foliage, and the bare poplars and tall cypress trees were lank sentinels etched against the melancholy skies.

Teresa immediately sought out her merchant friend, Ramírez, only to learn that he had died and that his brother had taken over arrangements. The brother had no house ready for Teresa and eventually he never carried through his deceased brother's plans. Meanwhile Teresa and her nuns had no place to live. The good widow, Luisa de la Cerda, hearing that Teresa was in the city, offered her home to the small band until accommodations could be found.

"You'll soon have a place," Luisa assured Teresa.

Facts proved otherwise. For almost three months no one was able to find a house for the nuns. At length another merchant friend promised to find a place for Teresa. She began plans for leaving Doña Luisa, but the merchant took ill and was unable to keep his promise.

Then, as if he had dropped from some dark Toledan cloud, a ragged young man who called himself Andrada appeared one day, asking for Madre Teresa. He was dressed in long black breeches and a red jerkin, with a broad silken sash about his waist, gypsy style. Sticking upright in his hat band was a stiff yellow feather. His manner was simple, but there was something audacious about the boy's lean, swarthy face with its gleaming white teeth and impish smile.

He presented himself to the nuns, saying that his confessor, Fray Martín, had told him to help Madre Teresa.

Teresa knew Fray Martín of the Cross, the Franciscan who had sent the boy, but was it safe to trust the youth?

"What we need is a house to live in," Teresa finally said, feeling that she had nothing to lose in revealing a fact already known throughout the city.

"A house? Madre wants a house?" He beamed Teresa a toothy grin. "Trust it to Andrada." He took off at once.

The nuns burst out laughing. "O Madre! What next?" A house!

Andrada returned in about three days. "Madre, I have your house." He made the announcement offhand, as if finding houses were routine procedure with him, and gave Teresa keys to a building that proved satisfactory.

What to put into the house after she had the convent established was Teresa's next problem. She later wrote to one of her prioresses about the Toledo convent. "For a while we had nothing for our beds but the pallets and blankets, and on that first day we didn't have even a piece of kindling wood to fry a sardine."

Teresa had the happiness of filling this Toledo convent

with nuns from her own foundations without having to draw on willing but less adaptable women from the Incarnation convent. She planned to remain here with the Sisters, to learn to know each of them better, and to help mold them to the new life of the Reform.

21

The evening meal was on the table. Teresa sat before her portion of bread and cheese. Two weeks ago this Toledo convent had not had wood " to fry a sardine"—had there been a sardine to fry. Now the nuns were already assured of their meals, frugal but sufficient.

As she broke her bread, Teresa listened to the quiet voice of Ana de los Ángeles reading the Scriptural passages for the next day's feast of Pentecost.

Clang! Clang!

Someone was ringing the large entrance bell. Sister Isabel went to answer.

"Madre," she whispered to Teresa on her return, "a messenger from Her Highness, Princess Ana of Éboli."

Teresa laid her bread on her plate. She surmised why the man had come. The one-eyed Princess had hinted at having a convent of nuns in her own summer villa in Pastrana, a small town northeast of Toledo. The messenger was probably here to present that request.

Teresa went to the parlor. She was right. The Princess was asking for a house of nuns, but Teresa was determined to refuse.

"Tell your Mistress that this house has been open only two weeks," Teresa said to him. "I'm not able to leave at this time."

The youth fingered the cap in his hand. "Madre . . ." he began, then hesitated.

Teresa saw that he was disturbed and, recalling her own negative reactions when meeting Ana six years before, guessed the boy's reason. He might be flogged if he returned without a favorable reply.

"When does your Mistress want me to come?" Teresa asked.

The messenger looked uncomfortable. "At once, Madre. I have her carriage to take you there."

Teresa glanced out the window. Before the house stood an ornate coach. The Princess was not asking; she was demanding.

Teresa called one of the nuns to give the youth his supper. "Take something to eat, *Señor.* I'll return." She left the parlor.

While the young man ate, Teresa went before the Blessed Sacrament.

"When do you plan to return to Pastrana?" Teresa asked the boy when he had finished eating and she had come back into the parlor.

"I won't travel on the feast, Madre, but early Monday morning."

The next day Teresa asked the advice of her confessor. It was the same she had received from her Sacramental Lord: "Go."

Teresa left Toledo, therefore, on Monday morning, taking with her two nuns. They spent the first night in a Franciscan convent of nuns at Madrid. As they entered the convent parlor, a familiar voice greeted Teresa.

"*Bienvenida,* Madre!"

"Doña Leonor!" exclaimed Teresa.

Besides founding the convent at Alcalá de Henares for María de Jesús and her small community, the devout spinster

119

had also established this convent of barefoot Franciscans next door to her home in Madrid, and she often spent time in the convent with the nuns.

Teresa was happy to see her friend again. After the evening meal, she and Leonor visited together for over an hour. Teresa told Leonor of her religious houses at Medina, Malagón, Valladolid, and Toledo. She also told her about the friars at Duruelo.

Leonor followed Teresa with interest. She was particularly curious about the friars. "Right now," she told Teresa, "I have two *señores* renting one of my houses. They are hermits looking for some hermitage connected with an Order— a new regulation of the Council of Trent, they say."

"Two hermits? Could I meet them?" Teresa was eager.

The next afternoon Doña Leonor took Teresa to see *Señor* Mariano Azaro, a brilliant engineer from Naples, and *Señor* Giovanni Narducci, a one-time apprentice to the painter Alonso Sánchez Coello.

Mariano answered Teresa's questions. "My companion and I can't find an Order suitable to the manner in which we are accustomed to living." He described their austere life.

Teresa outlined for the two men the Primitive Rule of the Reform. Mariano seemed interested, but he made no commitment. Giovanni seemed equally interested.

"Let us think about it, Madre."

Teresa promised to remain in Madrid a few days, waiting on their decision. The delay became unnecessary. Early the next morning the two men were at the convent door, asking for Teresa. "Madre," said Mariano, "we are accepting your offer to join the Reform." Then, smiling wryly, he admitted, "I can't understand my being so moved by the words of a woman."

Teresa laughed at his frank comment, but answered with quiet earnestness, "Our Lord alone moves hearts, *Señor*."

Teresa's next remark brought them to a practical problem. "*Señor,* what we need now is a house for you and your companion."

"God is with this venture, Madre. I have the promise of a house in Pastrana. A wealthy nobleman named Ruy Gómez, Prince of Éboli, has offered us . . ."

Teresa did not let him finish. "God be praised!" The thought of God's goodness overwhelmed her. "I'm now on the way to Ruy Gómez's villa in Pastrana to found a convent of nuns. If Ruy agrees, yours shall be our second monastery of Reform friars."

Ruy and Ana welcomed Teresa and the nuns. They also accepted the hermits and their idea of beginning a Reform Carmelite monastery.

Now that they were in Pastrana, Teresa realized that she could have delayed longer at Toledo. The house at Pastrana needed two months' renovations. Teresa and her nuns stayed in the palace with Ruy and Ana until the convent was ready. During this time Teresa sent for two more nuns to come from Medina.

On June 28, 1569, the new convent was officially inaugurated. It was a grand occasion, with lords and ladies present from the Court, and with a great show of processions, litanies, and singing. Everyone was happy—except Teresa.

22

Teresa returned to Toledo as soon as her nuns had been properly established in the new convent at Pastrana. From Toledo she sent Sister Isabel de Santo Domingo to Pastrana as Prioress. It would take a strong woman to withstand the interference of the Princess.

"That woman has caused me no end of worry," Teresa told Isabel. "Whatever you do, don't give in to her whims." Teresa was talking from experience. "She wanted me to accept as a novice an Augustinian nun who could not get along in her own community."

Teresa did not tell Isabel of the personal affront she had suffered at the hands of this one-eyed woman. The Princess had heard from some busybody that Teresa had written her life story, and Her Highness asked to read the book.

Teresa refused. The journal was the intimate account of God's work in her soul that she had written some years earlier while in Toledo.

Ana would not take no for an answer. She sent her husband, Ruy, to speak with Teresa about the manuscript.

"I assure you, Madre," Ruy said to Teresa in all good faith, "no one shall read the book but my wife and me."

It was more difficult for Teresa to refuse Ruy. He was the King's right-hand man, and if she fell from Ruy's graces, she might fall into disfavor with Philip II who until now had shown himself agreeable to her Reform. Teresa, therefore, reluctantly handed over a copy of her personal diary.

Soon everyone in the palace had read or heard of "Madre's book." Ruy was embarrassed. He apologized to Teresa, but the damage had been done. To add to the disgrace, those who read Teresa's expressions of love for God interpreted them on the level of courtly love and found the sublime account amusing.

"Be wary," counseled Teresa to Isabel.

Teresa remained in Toledo until August 1570. At that time she received a request to open a Carmelite convent in the university city of Salamanca. The petition came from the Jesuit rector of the college.

"You needn't worry about a house, Madre," he wrote. "A worthy man by the name of Nicolás Gutiérres has found a building for you."

With such bright prospects, Teresa started north for Salamanca. She took along one companion, Sister María del Sacramento, a somewhat older nun.

The weather was wretched. It rained most of the way and the roads were bogs. When the rain stopped, a cold wind set in. To add to her discomfort, Teresa had a toothache and her jaw was swollen and painful.

About noon on the eve of All Saints, the two nuns arrived in Salamanca with a group of merchants and traveling *hidalgos* who had joined them on the road. Teresa was disappointed to find that the house they had hoped to use was full of university students, a group of rowdy young men in no hurry to vacate their quarters. Teresa looked up Nicolás Gutiérres. He appealed to the owner of the building with whom he had made the agreement. After much ado, the youths moved out.

123

The building was far too large for a convent, and the students had left it littered. Teresa and María, in spite of their weariness, set themselves to cleaning the place.

The college rector heard of the nuns' arrival and sent two of his fellow Jesuits with food and blankets. The priests stayed and helped the nuns through the night, working to prepare a room where Mass could be said next day. When dawn broke on the feast of All Saints, November 1, 1570, Teresa rang a small bell, Mass began, and the Salamanca convent was a reality.

That morning Teresa sent a letter to Ávila for several nuns to come from St. Joseph's. The remainder of the day she and María continued cleaning the house. By evening they were worn out. Teresa stretched herself on a bundle of straw they had brought for beds and pulled a cover over herself. María kept roaming about the huge, empty house with a lighted candle stub.

"Madre," she answered when Teresa questioned her, "some of those students may have returned and be hiding in the empty rooms or under the stairways."

"We'll lock our door. There'll be nothing to fear," Teresa assured her without opening her eyes.

. . . I feel like laughing when I remember the fears of my companion . . .

The bells of the city were ushering in the feast of the Holy Souls when María finally settled down for the night. Teresa blew out her candle. A minute later María whispered from her corner of the dark room: "Madre, what would you do here all by yourself if I were to die tonight?"

Teresa sighed from pure exhaustion. "Sister, if that should happen, I'd think about it then. Now all I want is a little sleep."

The fifty-five-year-old foundress, the woman whose heart had been transfixed by a shaft of Divine love, who constantly lived in God's presence, turned over and dropped off to sleep like any humble, worn-out servant in Salamanca.

The Community remained in this house for about three years—I am not sure it is not four years, for my memory is not very reliable here, as I myself was sent to the Convent of the Incarnation . . .

23

It was May 1571. The sky over Ávila was brilliantly clear, the warm air was fragrant with the scent of blossoms, and birds sang from every branch and bush. All nature was unfolding under the magic touch of spring. By contrast Teresa's soul felt gripped in the chill of winter as she stood outside the convent of the Incarnation. She reached up and grasped the worn bell rope, gave it a sharp jerk and waited, dreading the moment that the door would open.

Standing beside Teresa was Padre Ángel de Salazar, the Carmelite Provincial who nine years ago had called Teresa to account for by-passing his authority in opening her first convent. Subsequently he had approved her work, but today he was angry with her. Salazar's mouth was set. Neither he nor Teresa spoke.

Less than six months ago Teresa had left Salamanca to open a convent at Alba de Tormes. From there she had hurried to Medina where Salazar was interfering with the nuns' election of a new Prioress. Teresa sided with the nuns against him. Shortly afterward she received a letter from him. "Madre Teresa, you are hereby appointed in obedience as Prioress in the convent of the Incarnation."

Teresa had cried over the letter. Could this be God's will? She had taken the letter to chapel, but Our Lord confirmed the Provincial's arrangement. "Go," He said to her, but His tone had been kind and compassionate. He assured her that the Reform would not suffer during her term of office at the Incarnation convent. Then He chided her lovingly for her lack of trust.

Now, pale but determined, Teresa stood outside the convent of the Incarnation, waiting for someone to answer the bell.

Salazar waited, too. From time to time he cleared his throat nervously. He blamed Teresa for the Medina nuns' refusal to accept the Prioress he had appointed. He ignored the fact that his action had violated the nuns' right to elect a Prioress of their choice. The Incarnation nuns had also brushed aside his suggestion of a Prioress. To punish both groups for their insubordination, Salazar intended to deprive the Reform of Teresa's presence and to humiliate the Incarnation convent by making Teresa their Prioress.

The door opened and Teresa and Salazar stepped inside. Lined along the narrow corridor on either side were all the nuns, pressing one upon the other. At the sight of Teresa an angry murmur rose. The grumbling grew as she passed along between the lines.

Teresa prayed silently, asking guidance for herself and acceptance from the nuns. "I can't blame them for feeling as they do," she said to the Presence within her.

It had been one thing for the nuns to reconcile themselves to Teresa's leaving them and opening a new convent; it was an entirely different matter for her to return and be set over them as their Prioress.

As Teresa walked forward, she read sympathy on some faces, but several women raised threatening arms when she came near to where they stood. Salazar kept himself between Teresa and the angry *señoras* and contrived to ward off their blows. He led Teresa first to the chapel and then to the large Chapter room. The crowd of nuns followed. They pushed

127

and shoved to get into the room. A party remained standing, milling about, muttering abusive remarks.

Salazar waited for the group to settle down, but the nuns took advantage of his hesitancy. The factions began shouting at each other. The bolder resorted to blows.

"Peace! Peace!" Salazar shouted and waved his arms to get attention. His efforts were futile. The situation had gotten out of hand. By now every nun was on her feet. The Chapter room was a madhouse.

Suddenly, in the midst of the melee, a nun fainted and fell heavily to the floor. Teresa was at her side at once. She knelt by the unconscious woman to keep her from being tramped on.

Teresa's spontaneous gesture had a distracting effect. The angry nuns stopped shouting. Salazar profited by the momentary silence to call loudly, "Will you consent to Madre Teresa as your Prioress?"

From somewhere in the disorderly group a clear, vigorous voice—that of Catalina Castro—responded. "Of course we consent. We love Madre Teresa."

Everyone was taken off guard. Heads turned to see who was speaking. Before the opposition was able to rally, Catalina's strong voice was intoning the *Te Deum Laudamus,* the hymn used at the installation of a Prioress.

The nuns who favored Teresa, but who had been intimidated by the opposing nuns, joined in singing the hymn. From somewhere near the rear door a nun appeared, carrying a processional cross. Despite the hostility, Teresa was led to the Prioress' chair.

The victory was not final. The Chapter—an assembly of nuns that would carry through the election procedure— would meet the next morning to settle the issue, and the rebels were determined that Teresa should not be chosen.

The dissidents huddled together in each other's cells that night after Matins and planned their strategy. They talked long after the bell had rung for the solemn silence.

When they returned to their rooms, the group had agreed that if Teresa de Ahumada did not voluntarily refuse the office of Prioress the next morning, they would bodily pick her up and carry her outside the convent walls.

Early the following day the community filed into the Chapter room. As each nun entered, she cast a furtive glance toward the Prioress' chair, then stared openly. A tall statue of the Mother of God, draped in a mantle of silk, stood on the chair, holding the keys of the house in her hand. To the right of the Virgin, in the Sub-Prioress' chair, was a smaller statue of St. Joseph. Teresa sat on the floor at the feet of the Virgin.

The rebellious nuns were taken aback. They glanced at one another, but before anyone could protest, Teresa, calm and smiling, rose and stood looking out over the assembly. Her eyes singled out one nun after another in gentle recognition. An awed silence took over. The nuns sat.

"My dear *Señoras*," Teresa began after acknowledging the presence of the Provincial. "It was not of my own choice to come to this house, and my heart goes out to each of you who, likewise, were not given a choice in this election and who are now being asked to accept as Prioress someone you do not like nor wish to obey. But Our Lord sent me here in obedience, and I trust that He will help me to serve you.

"Do not be afraid that I will inflict on you the Rule of the Reform. Your own Rule will be my guide. My only wish is for all of us to serve Our Lord in love. We are weak, but let our desires be great, and the merciful Lord will make our works equal to our desires."

Teresa had more to say, and she would eventually say it. Already the magnetism of her personality and her self-forgetting love had won over the opposition.

They were not evil women, these nuns. Most of them were simply frightened, afraid of being asked to do what was beyond their strength. Many, too, were testy only because they were hungry, starved for a decent meal. For the past five years at the Incarnation convent there had been no regular eating schedule for the simple reason that there was no regular food supply.

Teresa, with her penchant for the practical, took care to get food for the nuns before she made any attempt to lead them toward changing their lives. She sought out her wealthy friends and eventually gathered a little hoard of *reales* and ducats.

When meals were once more a routine part of the nuns' day, Teresa began to assume the authority rightly hers as Prioress. She went about this with tact and gentleness.

"My *Señoras* and Sisters," Teresa said to them one day. She spoke with exquisite kindness. "The hours we spend in the parlors chatting to no purpose are just so much time taken from conversation with Our Lord who longs to have each of us for Himself." Teresa was thinking of her own early life at the Incarnation convent.

The Rule had something to say on this matter, but it had been disregarded for so long a time that it was difficult for Teresa to re-establish its practice. By firm kindness she eventually managed to bring the pattern of constant visits to an end.

A young nobleman of Ávila who had formed a close friendship with one of the younger nuns was forever haunting the Incarnation parlors. He took exception to Teresa's stand on visits. He came one day, expecting to force the Rule in his favor.

The portress turned him away. "The Sister you wish to see is busy and will not be able to speak with you." Sometime later he returned and was given the same answer. Angry with the portress, the young *hidalgo* demanded to see Teresa. "I want to see the Prioress about this nonsense."

Teresa came promptly. She had been waiting for this opportunity.

The young man drew himself up with a show of importance before her.

"Madre Teresa, I'm a gentleman of rank. I'm not accustomed to the treatment I've been receiving at the Incarnation convent lately, and I don't intend to put up with it."

Teresa made no immediate response, and the young dandy continued his harangue, growing more heated. Teresa let him rant. When the irate nobleman ran out of words, Teresa answered quietly.

"*Señor,* from now on you will leave this convent in peace. If you continue to molest the nuns, I shall appeal to the King and have your head chopped off."

The calm threat coming from the veiled figure behind the grille had its effect. The grand *hidalgo* turned and disappeared out the door. The convent of the Incarnation never saw him again. Soon word got around that Madre Teresa would tolerate no nonsense, and the nuns at the Incarnation convent had no further difficulties with unwelcome visitors.

Teresa's next concern was the nuns' confessors. Mediocre or indifferent priests could tear down what she was laboriously trying to build. Teresa finally got the Apostolic Visitor, Pedro Fernández, to appoint John of the Cross as the nuns' confessor.

Teresa ordered built a small cottage, a simple hut, outside the Incarnation enclosure for John and a friar companion. John needed to be close if he was to hear the confessions of one hundred thirty nuns every two weeks and give them spiritual direction.

At first the *Señoras* distrusted the little friar. He was Discalced, a member of the Reform. They were afraid that he would give them severe and humiliating penances. But after a few nuns had confessed to the saintly priest, they spread the word quickly that "little Padre John" was "an angel." The nuns were glad to consult him and to follow his direction.

24

While Teresa worked to carry out her spiritual campaign of winning the nuns at the Incarnation convent to a more dedicated way of life, Philip II, King of Spain, was preparing to participate in an enterprise significant in European destinies.

In 1569, Selim II, or Selim the Sot, a dissolute Turkish Sultan, had captured Tunis from Spain. In 1571, he took Cyprus from the Venetians. It was clear to the entire Christian world that unless the Turk were stopped, the full length of the Mediterranean and possibly all Europe would eventually fall under Muslim domination.

Pius V, the reigning Pontiff, conscious of this threat to Christianity, organized the Holy League, a union of Rome, Venice, and Spain in May 1571. The purpose of the League was to unite the forces of the participating powers against Selim's advance.

By the end of summer the League had gathered some three hundred vessels and about eighty thousand men and set sail to encounter the Turk before the winter began.

It was agreed among the League members that Pius should have the last word in appointing a Commander-in-

Chief for the undertaking. The Pontiff met with the representatives of the League and a highly inflammatory discussion took place. Pius had hoped to assign Marc Antonio Colonna, a Roman admiral, as Commander-in-Chief of the expedition, but Venice fought to have a seventy-year-old sea veteran, Sebastiano Veniero, put in charge. In the end Pius appointed the twenty-four-year-old Don John of Austria, a Spaniard, to the position.

Cardinal Granvelle, a Spanish delegate, favorable to Don John, but recognizing him as a mere youth, protested. "But, Your Holiness, he's scarcely more than a child."

"Then a child shall lead us," remarked the Pontiff. History tells us that he acted under Divine inspiration.

Don John of Austria was the natural son of the late Emperor Charles V, and half-brother to Philip II, King of Spain. The young man had endeared himself to the whole of Spain by his winning manners and frank charm. In spite of his youth, he was a brave and daring leader who already had gained the military distinction of successfully suppressing the Moorish uprising in Granada a year earlier.

Shortly after his appointment as Commander-in-Chief, Don John set out with his fleet. He came upon the Turkish armada, under the command of Ali Pasha, in the Gulf of Lepanto (Corinth) about noon on Sunday, October 7. The story of what happened on that memorable day is one of Spain's boasts.

Ali Pasha's ships advanced in crescent formation, his right horn engaging Don John's left wing in a first attack. The Turkish ships outnumbered those of the Christians, but under the able leadership of their captain, Barbarigo, Don John's men proved a fair match for the numerous infidel and destroyed or took captive the Turkish vessels.

Don John's right wing, under the command of Giovanni Andrea Doria, fared less well and would probably have lost to the enemy if help had not come from the central division.

The major battle took place between the vessels in the central formation. Ali Pasha's flagship, the *Sultana*, bore down on Don John's smaller ship, the *Real*, and each opened fire with its heavy guns. When they drew close enough, the two flagships rammed each other with an impact that floored most of the men on both ships, but before the vessels had steadied themselves, Don John's men had grappled the ships together and for the next two hours the decks of the locked flagships became a single battlefield.

The fighting had begun at noon. At two it ceased with Ali Pasha's head on a pike and the Holy League's flag swaying in the breeze over the infidel flagship.

On October 27, news reached Rome that the Christians had defeated the enemy at two o'clock on Sunday, October 7. Monsignor Busotti de Bibiana, Pius V's secretary, pulled out his little black notebook and checked an entry made twenty days before: *Two o'clock, Sunday, October 7.* On that day Bibiana had been consulting with Pius V when suddenly the Pontiff got up from his chair, went to the window, opened it and stood looking out, motioning the bewildered secretary to silence. A few minutes later Pius closed the window.

"Let us discontinue our business as of now and praise God who has just given us the victory."

Bibiana left the room and once outside he jotted down the date and hour when the Pope had announced the Christian victory.

This incident is attested to in the canonization process of Pius V.

Pius V attributed the victory at Lepanto to the intercession of the Blessed Virgin Mary. The Confraternity of the Rosary had met in Rome and were praying Our Lady's beads when the battle was won. In thanksgiving, Pius instituted the feast of Our Lady of the Rosary and placed it on the calendar of the Church for October 7.

The battle at Lepanto was the last great sea battle fought with galleys, and it marked the beginning of the decline of Turkish maritime power. For the time it also put all Europe in awe of Spanish power and its Christian leader, Philip II.

25

Teresa's term of office at the convent of the Incarnation had not yet expired when, in February 1573, she received a letter from the Apostolic Visitor, Pedro Fernández, telling her to leave Ávila for a time and remove her nuns in Salamanca to a more suitable house in that city.

Circumstances forced Teresa to wait until July, but then she set out with Fray Antonio from Duruelo, Padre Julián, one other nun, and several youths who were among the company to help with the bags and bundles.

Julián insisted that they wait until dusk to get started. He knew from experience with Teresa that she could not stand the heat without getting ill.

Teresa allowed herself to be persuaded. When evening came, they started, each on a mule. A little donkey followed, loaded with bundles and household equipment.

It was dark before they came to the first stopping place. The road was full of ruts and Antonio's mule stumbled, throwing the Prior to the ground.

"Glory to God your skull is not split," said Teresa when Julián had helped Antonio to his feet and all of them had stopped to see how badly the Prior had been hurt.

To make matters worse, by the time the little group reached the village inn where they put up for the night, the donkey had disappeared.

"Madre," said Julián before he left Teresa and her nuns to go to his own sleeping quarters. "You might pray that we find the donkey. He's carrying all our money."

Teresa was not above twitting the chaplain. "You might have held off telling us that tonight, Padre, since we can't do anything about it until morning." But in her heart she was grateful for his concern.

Early the next day Julián sent a village boy to look for the missing beast. An hour later the lad returned, leading the donkey. The animal had been lying unharmed by the side of the road, a possible protest to the burden he had been expected to carry. The bundles and money were untouched.

The next evening they set out once more. When they reached the small town where they intended to stay for the night, Antonio left Madre Teresa and her companion in a dark street while he went to look for an inn. Julián and the youths had gone another direction for the same purpose.

Antonio came upon Julián and the young men.

"Where's Madre Teresa?" asked Julián.

"I told her to wait until I found the inn," said Antonio. "She's tired."

"I think we should get together again," said Julián. "The inn can't be too far away. Where did you leave Madre?"

"Three streets down, one over." Antonio directed his mule to lead the group through the dark.

When Antonio reached the place where he expected to find Teresa and the other nun, he could not locate them.

"Maybe it's a little further," he said. They rode on. It soon became evident that Madre Teresa and her companion were lost. There was nothing to do but wander about hoping to come upon the two.

Julián was annoyed at Antonio. He started to shout through the darkness. "Ma—a—dre! Madre Te-re-e-e-sa!"

The noise woke the villagers. Lighted candles appeared in the nearby cottages, and heads were thrust out windows to learn what was happening in the dark street.

After some thirty minutes, the group circled back to where Antonio had first met Julián. There in the dark they found the two nuns. When Antonio had not returned, Teresa had awakened a villager and promised him four *reales* if he could find her companions. The nuns could not afford to part with four *reales* but the man took them.

They reached the inn without any further mishap. The lodging was poor, and they were so crowded that they spent the night wishing for morning so they might leave the place.

On the fourteenth of August the group arrived at Salamanca. Teresa at once began to look for a house where she could transfer the Sisters from the unsuitable building they occupied.

It worried me a good deal to see what the sisters were suffering here—not for want of sustenance .. but because of their health, for the place was very damp and cold.

Before the end of the year Teresa found a place and firmly established the Salamanca community.

Teresa was now fifty-eight. She had opened a new convent in Alba de Tormes two years earlier, in 1571. Pedro Fernández, the Visitor, had hinted at the time that Alba might be her last foundation. On the other hand, a young widow, a sister to one of the nuns at Salamanca, was now offering a convent site and building at Segovia if Teresa would bring nuns to fill it.

Teresa took up the matter with Our Lord in prayer and was told to do as the Apostolic Visitor would suggest. To Teresa's surprise, Fernández directed her to accept the offer, and in early March 1574 she left Salamanca for Segovia, accompanied by Padre Julián and John of the Cross.

The city of Segovia lies eighteen leagues northeast of Madrid. It is a city of soft golden browns and yellows set against the blue snow-capped peaks of the Guadarrama. Long before the travelers entered the town they could see in the distance the graceful towering walls of the Alcazar, the town fortress, with its spires and turrets ablaze in the sunlight. Here in this fortified palace, four years earlier, Philip II had married Anne of Austria after the death of his beloved Queen Isabel of Valois.

The first Mass was said in the Segovia convent on March 19, 1574, the feast of St. Joseph. Teresa had very few nuns to place in the large house, but Providence was directing events that would provide a full community for the convent at Segovia.

Teresa returned to the Incarnation convent where her term as Prioress was expiring. The nuns were delighted to have Teresa back, and they voted to give her a second term. However, the Provincial intervened and allowed Teresa to return to the peace of St. Joseph's at Ávila.

26

Clang! Clang! Clang!

The gate bell at the Pastrana convent rang sharply and its echoes sounded ominous in the darkness. Waking with a start, the Sister-portress crossed herself devoutly, dressed with haste, and went to the door. She slid aside the small peep-panel. "Who's there?"

A husky, masculine whisper came through the opening. "I must speak to the Prioress at once."

"Who are you?" the portress repeated. She was unable to identify the person in the dark and suspicious of a visitor at two in the morning.

"Fray Baltasar from the Pastrana monastery."

Minutes later Baltasar was speaking with Isabel de Santo Domingo.

"Madre, I've come to prepare you. Ana, the one-eyed Princess, is coming here tomorrow to be a nun."

Isabel threw up her hands. "The Princess a nun! The Lord deliver this convent! What's happened?"

Baltasar spoke quickly. "Ruy Gómez died last night. Fray Mariano, from the monastery, was with him to the end. As soon as Ruy closed his eyes, Ana set up a weeping and wailing and declared that she was going to be a nun. She demanded then and there that Mariano give her the habit he was wearing. He protested, but . . ." Baltasar made a gesture of helplessness. "She put on the habit at once and told her family that she was leaving them to enter a nunnery."

The Princess' carriage pulled up before the convent gate shortly after eight in the morning. Ana had brought her mother and several maids. The women stepped from the carriage, Ana in her wrinkled friar's habit. For the next hour or so bundles, chests of clothes, and whatnots were carried into the two rooms that Isabel set apart for the Princess.

During the first few days Ana went about as meek as any novice. But the effort was too much for her. A group of ladies and grandees came to offer their sympathy over Ruy's death. Isabel told Ana that she could speak with them from behind the grille as was the rule.

"Why, Madre Isabel!" The Princess' dark eye flashed indignantly. "Indeed I will not! It's unthinkable. These are my dear husband's friends. They shall come to my room." The *señoras* and *hidalgos* entered the cloister and chattered noisily throughout the day.

Matters got worse. Eventually Isabel de Santo Domingo suggested to Ana that she return to her palace. The idea threw the Princess into a huff. "I have no intention of leaving this convent, Madre." She sulked for a week.

In an effort to compromise, Isabel gave the Princess one of the hermitages in the garden where Ana's friends could visit without interrupting the silence and solitude of the other nuns.

This went on for seven months. When Isabel saw that there was no way in which the Princess intended to conform to the Rule and that her presence would soon disrupt the entire community at Pastrana, she wrote to Teresa.

"Tell me what I am to do with this outrageous woman. I can't put her out of her own convent, and she won't leave."

"Then you leave."

Teresa's reply was more than a suggestion. She told Isabel that around the end of March she would send two men, Antonio Gaytán and Padre Julián, to remove the nuns and their belongings to Segovia.

Gaytán was a well-to-do layman, a widower, who became interested in the Reform and had once offered his services to Teresa for "whenever you need me, Madre." Teresa had accepted the offer and used him without scruple.

Isabel and the other nuns packed their bags and kept them in readiness. The Princess had suddenly gone back to her palace, but she continued to harass the nuns.

The end of March came. One day about noon, Antonio and Julián appeared at the Pastrana convent.

"Madre," asked Julián, "are the Sisters ready?"

"We could leave this minute," Isabel assured him.

"We'll wait until dark, but have everything packed. Antonio and I will come back around midnight. We can't bring the carts into the village—there are five of them—so each of us will have to help carry whatever you have."

"We'll be ready, Padre."

But five strange wagons suddenly appearing in the hilly woodland just outside Pastrana could not go unnoticed. Someone saw them and began to talk. How they guessed the purpose of the wagons is something to wonder at. Around midnight, when the two men and the group of nuns began to move quietly out of the dark convent, they suddenly found themselves surrounded by constables who prevented their leaving. About the same time Ana appeared, affecting to be highly offended.

Two hours of wrangling followed. The Princess finally consented to the nuns' departure on condition that Isabel accept one of Ana's maids into the fleeing community. Isabel agreed for the sake of peace, but she was determined to send the girl home if she proved unsuitable.

Ana continued to take the departure in bad grace. When she left the nuns to return to her palace, she was in a pouty mood.

It was two in the morning. The travelers could have remained until dawn since their departure was no longer a secret, but Isabel would not hear of it. She did, however, in spite of the unseemly hour, send Julián to summon a notary. In the presence of this official, Isabel placed into the hands of the constables all the jewels Ana had bestowed on the community, instructing them to return these gems to the grand lady. Isabel's action proved to be prudent when later Ana initiated a lawsuit against the nuns.

The group trudged out of the village, piled their belongings into the five carts, found themselves a seat among the bags and equipment and, along with the other drivers who had waited with the animals, started slowly moving forward toward the half-empty house in Segovia.

"Good Lord!" said Julián to Antonio as they started northward through the cold night. "What a stew that one-eyed woman can stir up."

Gaytán grunted. "Be at peace, Padre. Think what she might have done with two eyes."

27

Ten months after Teresa had removed her nuns from Pastrana she was on her way to open another convent at Beas, a small village in the province of Andalucía. Teresa was acting contrary to the orders of the Carmelite Provincial, who had specified that she was not to move out of the province of Castile, but she was unaware that she was going against his wishes.

> *. . . if I had known, when I went to Beas, that it was in the province of Andalucía, I should certainly not have gone there. The mistake I made was that, although the district itself is not in Andalucía . . . it is in the Andalucían province.*

Teresa had no natural liking for anything Andalucían. The province's climate, warm and humid, sapped her physical energy and had an effect on her spirtual vitality. She feared the place, too, overrun as it was by the riffraff bound for the Indies, who drifted through the countryside on their way to the Mediterranean ports. But two devout women, the Godínez sisters, had offered her a house in Beas and were asking to be accepted as postulants.

Accordingly, the first week in February 1575, Teresa set out from Toledo where nine nuns had gathered from several of her convents. Padre Julián and Antonio Gaytán accompanied them.

The men rode behind the creaking covered wagons that rumbled jerkily across the desolate, wind-swept plains of La Mancha and on toward the Sierra Morena range. Teresa and her nuns sat inside the wagons, huddled together under the sagging tarpaulins that kept flapping in the wind.

The trip south was uneventful until the wagon train reached the mountains. The mules dragged the cumbersome carts through the narrow passes and up the steep inclines. For most of the ascent the road skirted a precipitous drop of sheer granite that lost itself in a rocky ravine hundreds of feet below. The road grew more narrow, and the wagons inched forward.

To Teresa it seemed that they were getting nowhere. She drew aside an open end of the tarpaulin. From the look on the driver's face, she knew that something was wrong. She closed the canvas quickly. "Sisters, pray to St. Joseph. I think the driver's lost his way."

Teresa had scarcely finished speaking when, above the noise of the creaking wheels and the clomping hooves, a clear, strong voice rang up from the valley.

"Sto-o-o-p! Sto-o-o-p! If you go further, you will drop over the edge of the mountain."

The drivers brought the wagons to an abrupt halt, throwing the nuns forward on their low benches. Everyone climbed from the carts. The muleteers got down from their seats. Julián dismounted to take in the situation. He walked a few feet ahead of the wagons to where the road curved out of sight around the high wall to his left.

"Praised be God!" he gasped. Ten yards around the bend in the road they would have dropped into the abyss. He stepped to the edge of the road, shaded his eyes, and looked down to the valley floor. In the clear mountain air each tree and shrub seemed deceptively close at hand. He tried to see who had called the warning. But there was neither man nor beast in the valley. Cupping his hands around his mouth, Julián shouted.

"Where ... do ... we ... go ... from here? Where ... is ... the road?"

"Turn back," the voice answered. "The road is behind you. Turn to the left several hundred yards back." Each word came up from below with the clearness of a ringing bell.

Julián and Antonio walked back the way they had come. The stranger was right. A short distance behind them, the road turned to the left. The entrance had been hidden by some fallen rock that could be removed. With careful maneuvering the muleteers were able to back the wagons and get them onto the right road.

Teresa and her nuns got back into the carts. "Let's thank St. Joseph," Teresa said to them. "It was he who saved us." This narrow escape from a violent death had sharpened each one's awareness of the presence of God in their midst.

Before reaching Beas they had to cross the Guadalquivir River. The nuns braced themselves for this last ordeal. But heaven seemed bent on getting the journey over. According to Ana of Jesus, who was with the group and who left an account of the trip, the whole company suddenly found themselves on the further side of the river and entering Beas.

The townsfolk were waiting for the nuns at the gates, and they greeted the appearance of Teresa and her companions with shouts of welcome. The clergy were there, vested in their heavy brocaded robes, noblemen on caparisoned mounts formed a guard of honor, and the villagers, all in gala attire, crowded the streets. The entire populace led the nuns to the home of the Godínez sisters with song and music. A week after Teresa's arrival, on February 24, 1575, the convent was opened.

Unforeseen circumstances kept Teresa in Beas until

April. On the third of that month she met the man who, more than anyone else, was to figure both in her Reform and in her personal life, Padre Gracián.

Jerónimo Gracián de la Madre de Dios had recently joined the Reform at Pastrana. He was a Polish-Spanish priest, twenty-eight at the time, brilliant, learned, and prayerful. He was also handsome despite his receding hairline, chivalrous as a knight, and possessed of an almost hypnotic charm. Although he had made his profession of religious vows less than a year previously, Gracián had made such an impression on the Apostolic Visitor in the province of Andalucía, Padre Francisco de Vargas, that the Visitor had delegated his own authority to Gracián with power of visitation in the monasteries of the Mitigated and Reform Carmelites in Andalucía. This accounted for Gracián's presence in Beas.

Teresa was enchanted with this young priest. She wrote to the Prioress at Medina about him. "*O Madre mía!* You can't imagine how I have wished you were here with me these days. In my opinion, they have been the best days of my life, and I'm not exaggerating. Padre Gracián has been here with us more than twenty days, and as much and as often as I have talked with him, I have not begun to understand the worth of this man . . ."

Gracián's learning, his piety, and his enthusiasm for the Reform were qualities Teresa needed to weld her monasteries of friars. John of the Cross was a saint. Teresa had admitted as much. He was also very dear to her. But he had little grasp of the practical. Gracián, on the other hand, was holy without losing the ability to carry on business. The Reform needed an organizer who could bring some unity into the disparate autonomy that existed in the Reform monasteries.

O wisdom and power of God! How little we can do to escape His will! Our Lord saw well how necessary such a person was for this work which His Majesty had begun. I often praise Him for helping us in this; for, however ear-

nestly I had longed to ask His Majesty for a person who
would organize everything for our Order in these early
stages, I could never have asked for so excellent a person as
He gave us in this friar. May He be blessed forever.

But there was more to Teresa's liking of Gracián than
an appreciation of his fitness to govern her friars. She loved
him for himself, and with a sudden, deep emotion. She was
sixty, old enough to be his mother, and had only just met
him. Nevertheless, in less than three weeks she felt for this
young man the same possessive affection she might have felt
for a son of her own. She became concerned with all that affected him physically, mentally, and spiritually, and in a way
that was intense and personal.

Teresa realized that she would have considered an affection like this dangerous in one of her nuns, perhaps even in
herself at another period in her life, but with the clear-sight-
edness of those close to God, she knew that her love, though
warm and tender, was pure and without blame.

She spoke to Gracián of her soul, told him of the graces
God had lavished upon her, the visions, the ecstasies. It was a
joy for her to confide in him. He had that rare intuitive perception that makes communication by words almost unnecessary.

Teresa continued to be amazed at the qualities she saw
in Gracián. The month had not passed and she had taken him
for her spiritual guide. She vowed to obey his direction in all
matters not contrary to the obedience she owed God and her
higher superiors.

Gracián was in no less admiration of Teresa. He revealed to her his spiritual aspirations and his desire for a
deeper life in God. And he responded to her affection with a
candid, reverent love.

There was never anything unworthy in their conduct
toward each other, but the ill-disposed and evil-minded, who
watched for an opportunity to malign Teresa or her friends,
saw in the friendship a fertile field for sowing seeds of suspi-

cion about the character of the aging nun who had worn herself out in God's service and the balding, sensitive, but holy young friar who was her spiritual director.

Gracián made no attempt to justify his relationship with Teresa in the eyes of those who circulated vile accusations about him and Madre Teresa, but in an autobiographical section of a book he published after Teresa's death, he revealed with painful frankness how he felt.

"I want you to know," he wrote, "that she loved me very tenderly, and I loved her more than any creature on earth, after my own mother. But the great love that I had for Madre Teresa, and she for me, was very different from the love that is usually had in the world. That love is dangerous. It causes evil thoughts and temptations. It afflicts and puts a drag on the spirit, disturbing the sensuality. But this love that I had for Madre Teresa produced in me purity and love of God, and it gave her consolation and relief in her trials, as she told me so many times. Since this was true, I should not want even my own mother to love me more than Madre Teresa did. I bless God who gave me so good a friend. Now that she is in heaven, this love will not lessen, and I trust it will be of bountiful benefit! But what a thing is a vile tongue! When malicious people saw the great communication and familiarity between us, they judged that our love was not holy. But suppose Madre Teresa had not been as saintly as she was and that I had been the most evil man in the world, no one should have suspected wickedness of a woman sixty years old, and so cloistered and modest; as it was, we had to conceal this very intimate friendship to keep ourselves from being maligned."

28

Time proved that Gracián was too ingenuous to deal effectively with men less holy and more assertive who began to enter the Reform. In the 1585 Chapter of Elections held in Italy three years after Teresa's death, Gracián proposed a certain Padre Nicolás Doria as Provincial. Six years later this same Doria expelled Gracián from the Order. In 1595, however, a year after Doria's death, Gracián was reinstated among the Reform friars.

During his absence from the Order, Gracián was captured and enslaved by the Turks. They branded the symbol of the Cross on the soles of his feet. Gracián was finally ransomed and returned to Spain. He later went to Belgium to work for souls and he died there in 1614. He had lived thirty-two years after the death of the woman he had loved more than anyone else on earth, and he died invoking Teresa's name and clasping a relic of his saintly friend.

But, in 1575, the future was hidden from both Gracián and Teresa. At this time he was still her "dear son"—as he once signed himself in a letter to her—and she was his spiritual daughter who had vowed obedience to his direction.

It was in fidelity to this solemn promise that, in the

spring of 1575, she set off for Seville to found the eleventh convent of the Reform.

Gracián knew of Teresa's aversion to setting up another convent in the province of Andalucía, and he tried to placate her by giving her glowing accounts of the place, telling her that Seville was the richest city in Spain, that the nuns would lack nothing in alms, and that vocations would be plentiful among the devout *señoritas.*

Teresa's greatest concern was that she would be acting contrary to the Carmelite General's order forbidding her to open convents outside Castile. Gracián assured her that the powers of jurisdiction he had from the Apostolic Visitor superseded those of the General.

Teresa trusted his word and left for Seville at dawn on the eighteenth of May. Faithful Julián and Antonio Gaytán accompanied her as well as the six nuns who were to form the initial community.

By noon of their first day on the road, the heat had become stifling.

"We'll rest in the shade of the bridge ahead of us," said Julián, recalling how poorly Teresa could bear the heat.

It was a welcome idea to all, for the air inside the carts was oppressive, and the only consolation the nuns could find was in the thought that the fires of hell were worse.

They reached the bridge and scrambled down the embankment. There they were greeted by the grunts of half a dozen pigs that lay in the shade of the structure, their heaving bodies stretched along the muddy bank of the polluted stream. Antonio drove away the animals, but the fleas and stench remained.

The following day the company stopped at an inn. Teresa became ill with fever, and the hot sun, beating into the room where she lay, added to her discomfort. The nuns tried to cool her forehead with damp cloths, but the only water they could find was so warm that it made Teresa feel worse. Added to this was the noise all about her. Drunken men

150

brawled over their cups, and muleteers and merchants kept up a mixture of oaths and obscenities. Teresa asked to be taken back to the cart where it was quiet.

At length the group arrived at Córdoba. Teresa directed Julián to find a church on the other side of the river, away from the bustle of the city. They started over the bridge, but the axle shafts of the wagons were too wide. Julián was determined to make the crossing. He borrowed a saw from a friendly villager and set himself to trimming the shafts. It was a novel sight—a dusty Padre sawing on the axle rods of a lumbering wagon while the mules waited halfway on the bridge. Word got around. A group of youngsters from a nearby gypsy camp came running to get in on the fun. The bolder among them lifted the tarpaulin and stared at the nuns.

When Teresa and her friends reached the church where they expected peace, the feast of Pentecost was being celebrated with all the extravagant enthusiasm of the southern Andalucían temperament. Teresa wanted to push on without staying for Mass, but Julián persuaded her to remain, arguing the solemnity of the feast.

. . . as he was a theologian, we had to defer to his opinion.

Immediately after the service they took to the road again, preferring the heat to the wild carryings-on of the Córdobans.

They reached Seville on May 26. The orange trees were in bloom and the delicate fragrance of the frail white blossoms drifted under the heavy tarpaulins of the covered wagons where the nuns sat and mingled with the odor of their sweating bodies.

Inside the city, the small whitewashed houses, with their profusion of brilliant flowers, gleamed in the sunlight like alabaster urns overflowing with color. The streets echoed with gaiety, and the town square was filled with laughing

151

black-eyed youths and pretty *señoritas.* The sights and sounds brought back to Teresa memories of her romantic girlhood fancies, and she wished that she were back in Castile. She was much more in command of herself in the harsh, demanding climate of the northern province. She prayed that Seville's seductive beauty might not have enervating effects on the younger nuns who had come with her.

Fray Mariano, the "engineer" friar from Duruelo, was there to meet them. He had a house ready, but it was small and very damp, and the few furnishings that were in it had been lent by neighbors who promptly took them back before the nuns could replace them with their own equipment. For a while they were without a rope for the well, and for several days their only food was dry bread and apples.

Teresa could put up with this inconvenience, and her nuns were encouraged by her example. What she could not bear was a lack of frankness in those she loved. Only by much prodding did she discover why Mariano delayed saying the Mass that would confirm the public establishment of the convent. The Archbishop—Mariano finally let her know—while approving their coming, was against their living on alms alone. And this in Spain's richest city! Teresa went to see the prelate. After a drawn-out resistance, the ecclesiastic gave in to Teresa's wishes.

Teresa officially opened the convent at Seville on June 3, 1576. By then her brother Lorenzo had returned to Spain from Peru, and he had purchased a new home for the nuns.

Lorenzo had come back from the New World a wealthy man. He had married a daughter of one of the *conquistadores* in Peru, who after bearing him seven children had died at the age of twenty-nine. Lorenzo had brought with him his eight-year-old daughter, Teresita. She later entered the Reform and was Sub-Prioress at St. Joseph's in Ávila when she died in 1610.

Lorenzo had inherited some of his father's love for ostentation. When Teresa saw him for the first time on his return to Spain, she teased him for being a dandy. He had his hair cut short, longer in front and brushed forward above his forehead. In his left ear was a single gold earring. There was an orange-red plume in his hat and a row of gilt buttons down the front of his black doublet. His round mid-thigh breeches were of padded black velvet, slashed with gold silk to match his yellow hose.

Teresita was equally overdressed. The little girl was almost immobilized by layers of taffeta and silk, and her tiny fingers fanned out with a display of rings.

Teresa gratefully accepted Lorenzo's financial help, but she was weary with the delay caused by the Archbishop's tardy approval and wanted the opening ceremony of the new convent as quiet as possible. The Archbishop, very friendly by now, would not hear of it. He came in his flowing pontificals, accompanied by his clergy, and carried the Blessed Sacrament in procession. Friends sprang up from apparently everywhere, and the little house was filled with devout well-wishers.

At the close of the ceremony, Teresa knelt at the feet of the elderly prelate and asked his blessing. The old man placed his hands affectionately on the foundress' head. Then, to the amazement and edification of all, he knelt and asked Teresa to bless him.

It was while Teresa was at Seville that the nuns persuaded her to allow Fray Juan de la Miseria—Giovanni Narducci, one of Doña Leonor's former hermits—now in Seville, to paint her portrait.

Teresa posed for the picture, but after a few sittings she complained to her nuns. "Fray Juan says to me, 'Don't move your head, Madre! Don't shift your eyes!' Then he has me hold my hands together, just so. 'No, not like that, Madre. Higher, even with your shoulders.' He tires me no end."

The nuns were delighted with the finished portrait. Teresa looked at the painting and then at Fray Juan, standing by, pleased with himself.

"May God forgive you, Fray Juan," Teresa said, laughing. "After all I put up with, you painted me rheumy-eyed and ugly."

Teresa was ready to leave Seville. Before starting north she signed an agreement for a convent to be opened at Caravaca, not far from Seville. She delegated Ana de San Alberto as prioress and sent her with several nuns to open the new house.

Teresa then left Andalucía. She was happy to be going back to Castile, but she was returning under a shadow, and she had to struggle against a feeling of depression. A General Chapter of the Carmelites had met in Italy at Piacenza. Teresa's Reform had not been represented. Through some manipulative voting, a statement had been approved forbidding further establishing of houses according to the Primitive Rule. In the same Chapter Gracián and John of the Cross had been accused of grave misdeeds, and Teresa has been ordered to go to some convent in the province of Castile and remain there in inactivity.

> *. . . on no account to leave whatever house I should choose*
> *to live in—in other words, it sent me to prison.*

Teresa chose to go to the convent at Toledo. She went with her brother Lorenzo, his small daughter Teresita, and a group of friends among whom was a layman, Antonio Ruiz. Lorenzo had heard of Teresa's wearisome trip to Seville from Beas, and he also knew that she was hurting under her new assignment. He was determined that she should travel to Castile in comfort. At his own expense he hired coaches and provided plenty of food. When the weather was nice and the inn accommodations were poor, the travelers ate in the open fields, spreading their food on the grass under a tree. Once they ate in an old threshing barn and, in spite of her low spirits, Teresa wrote to Gracián of an amusing incident that happened there:

"We were having our noon meal in an old granary

when a large lizard darted inside my sleeve and up my bare arm. Thank God he didn't crawl in anywhere else. I think I should have died. It was bad enough as it was. . . . Lorenzo caught the lizard in no time and threw it from me, but Antonio Ruiz was standing by looking on and the lizard flew into his mouth. . . ."

29

Teresa had been in Toledo almost a year, reduced to silence and inactivity by order of the Carmelite General, when Gracián ordered her to write the book that was to become the most sublime of all her works, *The Interior Castle and Mansions.*

Teresa protested to Gracián that she was not competent, that a book such as he was asking should be written by a theologian. She feared that she would write poorly and lead others astray. Gracián, however, brushed aside her scruples.

Teresa, therefore, began to write a comprehensive treatise on the soul's journey through prayer to union with God. She began on June 2, 1577. In July of the same year she was allowed by the Carmelite General to return to St. Joseph's in Ávila. There, in September, she continued her writing.

Teresa says that it was God who showed her a very beautiful crystal castle with seven rooms or groups of rooms and Himself enthroned in the central room. He enlightened her on its significance. With His help she began to relate how the soul may enter this castle and eventually come to the great and loving King who rules it from within.

Prayer is the door to the castle. When once the soul enters through this, she finds herself in the First Room or Mansion. This is the room of self-knowledge, so necessary to fix the soul in humility. The soul moves about in this room in the dark, for the light from the central room does not penetrate here, or if it does the eyes of the soul are not yet able to benefit by the light. She is still very imperfect, dividing her affections between God and the world, willing and not willing the good, falling through weakness. Because grace has touched her a little, she is easily scandalized at the faults of others and her imprudent zeal sometimes antagonizes those she sets out to help.

After some progress has been made, the soul begins to practice mental prayer and bring herself to conforming more and more to God's will. By now, says Teresa, the soul has moved into the Second Mansion. Here her desires for God are authentic, but she struggles with her inability to maintain herself in recollection of spirit and she continues to fall into venial sin. Nor does she avoid the occasions of sin. However, if she perseveres in mental prayer, God in His mercy will draw her through the Second Mansion into the Third.

A soul who enters the Third Mansion is more sensitive in her relationship with the Divine Owner of the castle. She is careful to avoid venial sin, to practice penance, and to do works of charity. She becomes more prudent in her speech. Her prayers are more simple, and she feels the stirring of a Divine hunger.

Until now the soul has been engaged in discursive thought and meditation, working almost always with the intellect. In the Fourth Mansion she begins to think less and love more. The will is active. The love is not a matter of tender words but a firm resolve to avoid sin, to please God in all one does, to desire God's glory and the welfare of the Church.

The gift of prayer granted to the soul in this room is a supernatural experience not dependent on the soul's activity and therefore not at her command. It comes when God gives it, and nothing the soul does can obligate God to bestow it.

A blessed fact! For if we were repaid in proportion to any of our works, God would always be obliged to give us less than Himself.

If her nuns hope to be admitted to this Fourth Mansion and experience this gift, let them remember that the best preparation for receiving it is humility. Teresa never forgets, nor does she let others forget, that the surest way to draw God into the soul is to realize one's own unworthiness of the Divine favors.

The true union with God that begins in the Fourth Mansion becomes more perfect in the Fifth. This union transforms the soul and affects the body. The senses and faculties are suspended. At times the person loses consciousness and appears as though dead.

This experience of union with God may happen to the soul but once. Nevertheless, the soul never doubts, when the prayer is over, that she was truly united to God, since even the remembrance of the experience is so deeply engraved in her memory that years afterward the soul can recall with clarity the impact of her close encounter with God. If this certitude is lacking, she may be sure that she has not been wholly united with God even though she has experienced a Divine benefit.

God initiates this union, entering the soul without the action of the will or other faculties. Yet even if the effort of the soul is not the source of the prayer, the soul can dispose herself for this favor by humility. She can also assure herself that she has not been deceived by the devil or deceived herself if, after the prayer has passed, she is filled with a desire to praise God, to do penance, to seek solitude, and to become the "slave" or servant of all. This charity toward others is the touchstone of authentic prayer.

Teresa was writing to her Sisters and her admonitions were always practical: Do not think you need do big things, Sisters. There are countless small ways by which you can show your love for others: hiding their faults; rejoicing in their good fortune; doing what they want done even when it means giving up your rights; putting their good before your own; taking on some work that they may be relieved of it. All this will cost, but it is in this way that the soul grows in charity. Without an effort to do this, the soul is not assured of progressing in prayer.

In the Fifth Mansion the soul also begins to suffer. But Teresa assures her daughters that it is God Himself who will support them and in so effective and loving a manner that they will desire suffering, seeing it as a necessary part in God's plan for their purification. But the sufferings will be real. Good people will begin to find fault with the soul who has set out to seek God; enemies will do their best to make her appear foolish and insincere; physical illness will weaken the body; timid and inexperienced confessors will cause the soul to doubt and become fearful. All this is the beginning of a pattern of suffering that continues into the Seventh Mansion. But through it all God bestows great fortitude and patience.

As Teresa continues to tell of the soul's movement toward the Divine union, she searches for some apt comparison to describe the growth of love between the soul and God, and likens it to the development of love between man and woman. The graces of union that the soul receives in the Fifth Mansion are like the initial meeting between two lovers, like their first deep exchange of confidences and feeling.

But if the Fifth Mansion can be compared to this beginning of the love between two human hearts who someday hope to share themselves in a more intimate way, the Sixth Mansion can be considered a time of betrothal or engagement.

In this room or mansion the Divine Lover showers gifts on His betrothed: perfect self-knowledge, profound humility, an understanding and knowedge of the majesty of God. These gifts, however, become a source of acute pain to the soul, for, seeing herself so vile and God so great and desir-

159

able, she agonizes in a need to flee herself and to embrace Him. Her desires consume her like a fire, at once sweet and painful.

This pain is not a lasting state. It comes suddenly and is of short duration—a blessing, since the soul could not bear up under its burden for long without a miracle. Yet because of the intense pleasure caused by the pain, the soul desires its return. Nor does the soul lose her peace or begin to doubt that the favor was from God since the pain proceeded from the center of the soul to which the devil has no access, and the movement was all from a source other than the senses or faculties of the soul.

The effects of this experience also point to God as its origin. The soul is determined to suffer more for God and to withdraw as far as possible from all earthly satisfactions. She becomes foolish in her love, desiring to have a thousand lives to employ for God's glory. She is "madly" in love with the Divine.

30

Teresa took out time while speaking of the Sixth Mansion to explain to her nuns the difference between an intellectual and an imaginative vision.

Intellectual visions may last a long time—a day, a week, a year. Imaginative visions pass like a sudden flash of light. One "sees" nothing in an intellectual vision, but the soul's certitude is so great that she has no doubt of the vision's reality.

Teresa's vision of Christ's continuous presence at her side was an intellectual vision. She knew He was there as one knows the presence of another in a darkened room, but she saw nothing.

The soul is thrown into a state of happy confusion and humble gratitude at the favor bestowed upon it. When the vision leaves, often as abruptly as it began, the soul is unable to bring it back. But she can rest secure that she has not been deceived when she considers the effects in her life. She is incited to a more tender love of God, she desires to be more totally surrendered to Him, and she strives for a greater purity of conscience.

In an imaginative vision God may show Himself in His

Sacred Humanity, or it may be some Saint that appears to the inner eye of the soul. Something is truly seen but not with the eye of the body. The vision is swift but distinct. The grandeur of the Sacred Humanity seen thus is so overpowering that such a vision occurs only when the soul is in rapture, out of its senses, for otherwise she could not endure such extraordinary majesty.

Anyone who thinks she has an imaginative vision of Our Lord and who finds herself lingering over the sight a long time, or who does not feel overwhelmed by the supreme dignity of the Divine Person, is not seeing a true celestial vision but is being led by a play of the imagination. Neither does one work up to such a vision. The soul has not thought of such a thing happening when suddenly it is there.

Such a vision leaves the soul instructed in so many truths and filled with such humility and fortitude that it is impossible afterward to think that the vision may have come from the devil.

Teresa warns her nuns against desiring imaginative visions. Such a desire flows from a lack of humility and misunderstanding of the importance of God's will in their regard. How do they know this is the path God wishes them to walk? And have they the fortitude to suffer the trials endured by those to whom these favors are granted? Are they aware that the devil can present such a vision or that their own imaginations can make them see what they want to see?

In the Seventh Mansion the soul is brought to the spiritual marriage. She can truly say now, "For me to live is Christ." In this mansion the soul is admitted into the continual companionship of the Blessed Trinity and becomes one with God in a union unsurpassed except by those enjoying the Beatific Vision.

Any union of the soul with God prior to this one can be compared to the joining of two candles whose lights may be united to make one flame. The candles can be separated again and the flames parted. In the spiritual marriage the soul is like a drop of water falling into the ocean. It can no longer be withdrawn but has become one with the water of the sea.

The soul's awareness of the Trinity is sometimes less clearly felt than at others or she would find it impossible to undertake any work. But whenever the soul is left to return to her inner being, she finds this Divine Presence waiting there to embrace her. Even while engaged in work, a part of her never leaves the side of the Divine Guest.

The soul continues to experience suffering in this mansion, but she becomes indifferent to either suffering or its absence. Her one longing is that the will of God be done in her, whether by suffering or joy, by life or by death. If the choice were left to her, she would desire to live many years provided that it would mean more glory to God. She has, in a sense, disappeared. God alone is. "I live now, not I, but Christ lives in me."

There is complete transformation, ineffable and perfect peace; no higher state is conceivable, save that of the Beatific Vision in the life to come.

Souls that have been granted the favor of Spiritual Marriage are not confirmed in grace, and they may not relax their vigilance even though their position is more secure. The need to be on guard is an aid to keep the soul humble and to help her better understand what a great favor God has given her.

The soul admitted to the Divine nuptials must realize, above all, that this delight is not for her alone. It is meant to be poured out in love on others. This is what the Spiritual Marriage is all about: that from it may be born good works. And lest her Sisters feel that the cloistered nature of their lives handicap their doing good deeds, Teresa assures them that the Lord does not consider the greatness of their acts, but the love with which they are done.

Who sweeps the floor with high intent
Makes that the action fine.

George Herbert, *Adapted.*

Teresa had written *The Interior Castle and Mansions* to blaze a prayer trail for the spiritual daughters and to arouse in them a desire to follow. At the same time she was aware that some of her nuns would need to study their hearts and sort their desires.

Did her account of the castle and its mansions make her daughters eager for visions and extraordinary favors? If so, they had missed the point. Visions and special spiritual favors are not necessary for holiness.

Had the reading of the book made them hunger for mystical contemplation? Good. Let them foster that longing. But were they willing to be humble, to order their lives toward receiving this great favor? Even so, they are not to forget that mystical prayer is a free gift of God—may His Majesty be pleased to grant it to them!—but it, too, is not essential to sanctity.

Among the desires awakened in their hearts by what she had written for them, had they discovered a deep, sincere yearning that God's Will be done in them at no matter what cost? Did every other favor from God seem less desirable than the gift to want only and always and everywhere what God willed? If this is what they learned from reading *The Interior Castle and Mansions*, God be praised! Surrender to God's Will is the surest and safest and sweetest road to genuine holiness.

Teresa had begun to write her book on prayer in July 1577. She finished it on the eve of the feast of St. Andrew, November 29. During the same month the nuns at the Incarnation convent were preparing to elect a new Prioress. They sent word to Teresa, asking her to accept the position. She refused, since she was still under the Carmelite General's displeasure and bound by his order to remain inactive.

Doña Ana de Toledo was finally put into the office, against the desires of the majority of nuns. Teresa was not present for the election, but from a letter she wrote to the Prioress of Seville, it was evident that she knew what had taken place.

"I don't believe anything like what I'm going to tell you ever happened before at the convent of the Incarnation," she wrote. "The Provincial of the Calced came to Ávila two weeks ago to be present at the election. He threatened to excommunicate any nuns who voted for me. But the nuns didn't pay any attention to him. Fifty-five of them voted for me anyway.

"As each Sister handed her written vote to the Provincial, he looked at the ballot, and if it was for me, he excommunicated the Sister on the spot and scolded her severely. Then he pounded on the table, tore up the votes, and burned them. . . .

"The next day he called together the nuns who had voted for me. He was going to hold a new election. They told him it was unnecessary since they had already voted. When he heard this, the Provincial excommunicated them again, and, calling the rest of the nuns, forty-five of them, he declared a new Prioress elected. . . .

"The nuns who voted for me say they consider the new Prioress just a temporary vicaress. . . . I do not know how it will end."

31

The election fiasco at the Incarnation convent indicated the growing tension between the Calced and the Discalced begun after the General Chapter in Piacenza. Much of the antagonism was a natural resentment. Those living under the Mitigated Rule saw the Reform as a rebuke to their way of life.

But ill will toward the Reform was not confined to the Calced. Every lax monk, priest, prelate, or nun throughout Spain saw in Teresa's efforts toward religious renewal a personal accusation and, indeed, a judgment on the moral decadence of the entire Church.

The list of sixteenth-century canonized saints reads like a litany, but alongside examples of remarkable holiness was the presence of moral decay from the Papal throne to the poorest peasant's hearth. During Teresa's lifetime she saw the See of Peter held by unworthy men, one who had fathered four bastards. Ecclesiastical offices were sold to the highest bidder, and the cardinal's hat was bestowed on mere boys, usually relatives of the Pontiff.

Many of the clergy were ignorant. Only two of every hundred were able to understand the Latin liturgical books.

Among the monks were lazy, dissolute men. Mendicant friars roamed the countryside taking advantage of the illiterate and superstitious laity and exploiting the poor. Many nuns were unfaithful to their vow of chastity.

In Teresa's own convent of the Incarnation there had been abuses. Some of the nuns held clandestine meetings with their gentlemen friends. Many wore jewelry or added extra frills and pleats to their religious habits. Those who could afford it had luxurious furnishings in their cells, and the poor nuns fawned on the rich of the town.

Even before Teresa's conversion to a more fervent life, she had deplored these evils and taken no part in them. Later, in an effort to curb such excesses, she advised parents to marry their daughters to some respectable *hidalgo* rather than place them in a convent of relaxed religious discipline where each nun becomes a temptation to the other.

The faith of many was tested by the religious malaise of the times. Some who looked on with concern, like Ignatius of Loyola, the saintly founder of the Jesuits, stayed within the Church and helped to better her by reforming their personal lives. Others, like the Augustinian monk, Martin Luther, embittered by the betrayal of religion in high places, left the Church, but they occasioned by their rebellion the calling together of the Council of Trent with its lasting effects on Church discipline.

With all Christendom in need of reform, but balking at the suggestion, it was only to be expected that antagonism should break out between the two "families" of Carmelites, the Calced and the Discalced, when one group began to lead a more regular life. Even so, hard feelings would probably have burned themselves out over a period of time if the Reform friars had shown themselves less aggressive toward the Calced. Ironically enough, the man who spearheaded this aggression was none other than Gracián.

Using the faculties he had received from Francisco Vargas, the Apostolic Visitor, Gracián proceeded to found monasteries outside the province of Castile. This was contrary to the orders that Teresa had received from the Carmelite General, Giovanni Rossi, when he had approved the Reform. Gracián was also agitating to separate the Discalced from the original Carmelite Order or at least to set them up as an independent province.

In all this activity, Gracián argued that his power, delegated to him by Vargas, came from the Holy See and superseded the power of the Carmelite General. Whether or not he had a point, he made no effort to defer to Rossi. Teresa feared this willfulness on the part of Gracián and urged him to communicate with the General and explain his position. But Gracián had his moment of stubbornness and blundered on.

The Calced became more hostile. Some monasteries refused Gracián admittance when he came for canonical visitation. Matters went so far that Teresa made Gracián promise never to take a meal at a Calced monastery. She feared that the Calced might poison him.

While Teresa fretted about Gracián, news reached her that, under cover of dark, a group of Calced friars had broken into the little cottage behind the convent of the Incarnation where John of the Cross was living with a companion friar, Padre Germán. The intruders carried off the two priests.

Teresa was angry and upset by the news. She immediately wrote to the King, begging his help for the release of the captives. This was not her first correspondence with Philip. She had written to him on another occasion regarding his spiritual condition. "Do not forget, Sire, that King Saul was also anointed; nevertheless, he became a castaway." Teresa appealed to Philip now as to a friend of the Reform. "I should prefer having the two friars fall into the hands of the Moors," she informed him.

The priests had been kidnaped on the night of December 3. By Christmas Eve Teresa still had not heard of their whereabouts. She was on her way to the chapel for Compline, thinking of John and praying for him, when a gust of air blew out her candle. She missed a step and fell down a flight of stairs, breaking her left arm. The fracture troubled her the rest of her life.

"The devil probably had a hand in this, but I was glad to offer the pain for Padre John," she confided to Sister Ana de San Bartolomé who was with her at the time.

This nun, born Ana García, played an increasingly important part in Teresa's life. She had been a shy peasant girl when she asked admittance as the first lay Sister into the convent of St. Joseph at Ávila in 1570. Teresa had been so charmed by the young woman's simplicity and good sense that she later made Ana her secretary. After Teresa broke her arm and was unable to dress herself, she took Ana with her wherever she went. Ana died in 1626. In 1917 the Church beatified this humble woman.

Winter ended and spring changed into summer, but no report reached Ávila concerning John. Then, in the middle of August, a story came from Toledo.

About five o'clock one morning there was a rapid knocking at the Toledo convent door. The portress opened the peep-panel. In a flash she was back at the Prioress' door, breathless with excitement.

"It's Padre John of the Cross!"

Ana de los Ángeles hurried to the door and brought the young friar into the parlor. "God be praised that you're alive, Padre." Then she saw, with horror, that there were blotches of fresh blood on his ragged, dirty clothes. "You're hurt!"

John shook his head. "Don't worry, Madre. Find me a place to hide. They'll search for me as soon as they find I'm missing."

"They? Who?"

"The Calced."

"Here in Toledo?"

John nodded.

Ana's mind worked quickly. She knew that the Rule forbade even a priest to enter the nuns' cloister without a valid reason. But, thanks to God, there was a sick nun in the infirmary waiting for an opportunity to go to confession. That was reason enough. Ana unlocked the cloister door and John entered.

In the meanwhile, across the city, the friars in the Calced monastery were running about shouting to each other, "Padre John is missing!"

"Impossible!" said the men responsible for guarding the little friar. They went to his cell, a cramped dungeon scarcely large enough for a man to turn around in. The friars pulled open the door. The lock fell into their hands, and the screws clattered onto the floor.

While they stood looking into the empty cell, a friar came running from the garden. "A rope is hanging from the gallery window."

So that was it! An inside job. Who had given him the rope? But when they examined it, the rope was made of strips from John's blanket.

"He can't be far away," said the friar in charge of the garden. "The rope was ten feet too short and the ground below is rocky."

A half-dozen friars hurried to the garden and searched the shrubbery, hoping to find the prisoner lying somewhere with broken bones. They were infuriated when it became clear that John was nowhere about. At once they sent two of their number to the Toledan convent.

The crafty portress listened while the two friars explained their presence. She handed them keys to those parts of the house not under cloister. "I should think it would be a miracle if you were to find Padre John in our house without our knowing about it, but you may look."

The sick nun in the infirmary took her time confessing, unaware of her role in the game that was being carried on. After she had finished and the two Calced friars had gone back across the city to their monastery, the nuns brought John a dish of warm, stewed apples flavored with cinnamon. While he ate, they bustled about, heating water for him to bathe and bringing him fresh, clean towels and plenty of soap. The Sister sacristan brought him a soutane and the laundress gathered up his dirty clothes. What happy excitement there was in their house that day!

Ana sent word to the administrator of the Holy Cross Hospital, a friend of the nuns. That evening he came with his carriage and took John with him, hiding the friar in the hospital for the next two months until it was safe to send him to the nearest house of the Reform friars some distance south of Toledo.

Several months passed before Teresa saw John. They sat on either side of the grille in the parlor at St. Joseph's and talked. He was "so thin and covered with so many scars that he seemed an image of death," Teresa later wrote to one of the nuns.

John told Teresa of his imprisonment and how the Mother of God had appeared to him and instructed him on the way to escape. The holy friar did not blame anyone for the way he had been treated. Teresa, on the other hand, found it hard to control her feelings. "I can't understand how God allows such things to happen." For nine months the Calced had fed the young friar nothing but bread and water; they had scourged him daily, deprived him of visitors, refused him water to bathe, and given him no change of clothing.

After John left, Teresa talked about him to the nuns. "I truly envy him. Isn't it marvelous that Our Lord found him courageous enough for such terrible suffering?" Teresa's hot Spanish blood had had time to cool and the saint in her won out against her natural inclination to wonder why "God allows such things."

32

John's imprisonment, the ill-will of the Calced against Gracián, and her forced inactivity were a heavy cross for Teresa. Added to this she now felt herself losing the support of "those blessed men of the Company [the Jesuits]" who had always stood by and upheld her.

In 1572, Teresa had refused to accept into her convent at Valladolid a one-eyed candidate (not the Princess) recommended by Jesuit Father Jerónimo Ripalda. In writing about this to Doña María de Mendoza, the co-sponsor of the Valladolid convent—who also wanted the one-eyed woman accepted and may have urged the request as "a favor" to the Jesuits—Teresa replied, "They [the Jesuits] wouldn't accept an unsuitable postulant for *their* Order as a favor to *me.*" But this difference of opinion could hardly have alienated the Jesuits as a group or even Ripalda as an individual since a year after this disagreement Teresa chose Ripalda as her confessor at Salamanca and in obedience to him wrote an account of the founding of her convents.

Another unfortunate incident that for a time strained relations between the two Orders had to do with the inheritance of a certain Casilda de Padilla who entered Teresa's

Reform and later left. Casilda's inheritance would have been a financial boon for the Valladolid convent. However, when Casilda left the Reform, her money went with her. Casilda's older brother was a Jesuit, and Teresa thought she had reason to suspect that some Jesuit had a hand in Casilda's leaving the convent. Whether this was true, appearances made it easy for Teresa to think that not everything had been above board and that the money had gone to the Jesuits who were building a college at the time.

A further disagreeable situation arose when it was rumored that Jesuit Father Gaspar de Salazar, a staunch supporter of Teresa, was leaving the Company and joining the Reform. Salazar was a man of merit in his Order, having held various important positions. The idea that he might be considering a change over to the Discalced set up violent reactions. In the end he remained in the Society and the rumor came to nothing.

Some individuals both in the Company and in the Reform may have held grudges on this matter, but once it was over, Teresa considered it past. A month after the Salazar story died down Teresa was writing about her soul to the Jesuit rector at Ávila, her spiritual director at the time. She also instructed Mariano, the friar at Pastrana who formerly had been an engineer, to help the Ávila Jesuits fix their faulty water supply equipment.

With all these precedents, however, it is easy to understand why she felt she was losing the support of "those blessed men" when she received a letter from the Jesuit Provincial in Castile, informing her that the priests of the Society would no longer be confessors to the Discalced nuns.

The decision came at an opportune time. There were over two hundred friars in the Reform by now. These could hear the confessions of the nuns. As for the Jesuits, their apostolate in the Church involved moving about wherever the Pope might call them to serve. If the Fathers of the Society tied themselves down to being fixed confessors of the nuns, they would limit the mobility necessary for their work.

Nevertheless, the situation was full of emotional overtones, and it was inevitable that someone's feelings be hurt. That the decision came from the Jesuits probably jarred Teresa more than if she had made the proposal.

Teresa had just come through this change of relationship with the Society of Jesus when her worries about Gracián began again. On more than one occasion Teresa had chided Garcián on his lack of frankness with her in handling matters of the Reform. Now she heard that he had called a Chapter of the Discalced without permission of either the Pope or the Carmelite General and had set up the Discalced as a separate province with old Padre Antonio de Heredia at its head.

Almost simultaneously with this information came the report that Felipe Sega, the Papal Nuncio to Spain, had dissolved the illegally established province and had imprisoned Gracián in a Calced monastery at Alcalá de Henares, imposing penance upon him and ordering him to cut all ties with the Discalced.

Teresa had praised God for the way John of the Cross had borne his imprisonment. She felt less confident that Gracián could hold up under prolonged persecution. Her fears were confirmed when word spread that Gracián had defected to the Calced.

She wrote to him at once: "Padre, stand firm for the right, even if it puts you in danger. I am not surprised that some who say they love Your Paternity are trying to remove the suffering from you, but you would prove yourself an unloving son to abandon Our Lady in these difficult times. . . . God keeps us all from doing such a thing. . . .By leaving the Discalced you would not escape trials, but involve yourself in greater ones. By God's help your present trials will end; if you choose to join the Calced your trials would perhaps last a lifetime. Let Your Reverence think about this."

Gracián's mother, Doña Juana Dantisco, wrote even stronger words to her son: "I am hearing that you wish to leave the Order of Our Lady. If such a thought has entered your mind, don't ever speak to me again. Don't write to me, or even regard me as your mother. I don't want a son who is so cowardly that a little suffering makes him turn his back on such a Mother as Blessed Mary and leave the Order to which he gave himself so wholeheartedly and to which I also dedicated him."

A friend of the Reform at the Court, the Count of Tendilla, was so disgusted when he heard that Gracián might join the Calced that he went to the monastery where Gracián was held prisoner. "What's this I hear about your wanting to abandon the habit of Our Lady of Carmel, Padre?" he asked, fingering a weapon. "If that's the case, I've vowed to run you through with my dagger."

Gracián regarded the Count's nervous finger on his blade. "It's a lie," he said. "The Calced have started the rumor to blacken my name."

The nobleman looked dubious, but when Gracián refused help to escape, the Count agreed that he had been misinformed.

The year 1578 was drawing to a close. It had been a difficult period for the Reform. John of the Cross had been imprisoned; relations with the Jesuits had been strained and unpleasant; Gracián had fallen into the hands of the Calced; Teresa herself was undergoing interior trials and was troubled with doubts and misgivings.

The day before Christmas she sat praying in her cell when the portress knocked at her door. "Madre, several ecclesiastics to see you."

Half an hour later Teresa was back in her room with a copy of a Decree from Felipe Sega, the Nuncio, in her hands. She went to her knees and reread the words the envoys had declared to her minutes before. There was no mistaking the message. The Reform was being taken out of her hands. The Discalced nuns and friars were henceforth to be under the direct jurisdiction of the Calced Provincial and Superiors in both the province of Castile and Andalucía. While the Decree did not state explicitly, it implied that Teresa would be transferred to a Calced convent. As of now she was to discontinue all correspondence with Padre Gracián.

The shock of this unexpected turn of events was more than Teresa could bear. She let the document slip to the floor, covered her face with her hands, and cried. All afternoon she stayed alone in her cell, weeping and praying. She could think of nothing but self-reproach. Her doubts and misgivings had been confirmed. The Reform was falling to pieces, and it was her fault. She had let herself be deceived and had deceived others.

When Teresa came to the table for the evening collation, her eyes were red and swollen. Sister Ana de San Bartolomé tried to persuade her to take some food, but Teresa turned away. Then, as if Christ could not bear that His loved one should be in so much pain, He suddenly appeared at her side—we have Ana's word for this—took a piece of bread, blessed it, and held it to Teresa's lips. "Eat this for My sake," Ana heard Him say to Teresa. Teresa took the morsel, but when Christ left her side, she was once more desolate and she cried softly throughout Christmas Midnight Mass. There was no bitterness in her soul, but she shared some of the abandonment her Lord had known on the Cross.

33

If the year 1578 was bitter for Teresa, it was equally so for Spain and particularly for King Philip. During this year Don John of Austria, Philip's half brother, who had served him so well at the battle of Lepanto, died at the age of thirty-one. Prior to this Philip became entangled in a murder plot that left him disillusioned with his trusted secretary, Antonio Pérez, and cost the monarch his peace of soul for the remainder of his life.

Philip had sent Don John to Flanders in 1576 as Captain-General to calm the unrest in the Lowland countries. John left Spain disguised as a servant of a nobleman, dressed in rough homespun and with his hair and beard dyed.

News of this deceit had even filtered into the cloister, and Teresa wrote to the prioress at Valladolid, her niece, María Bautista, ". . . pray to God for Don John of Austria, who recently set out for Flanders in disguise."

Philip was determined to win Flanders by a policy of peace, but William, Prince of Orange and one-time member of the Spanish council in the Lowlands, had defected from Spanish loyalty and stirred up the Lowlanders. Don John found William an enemy and had to defend himself and his position against him by force of arms. To effect this he needed money and men, and he sent his trusted secretary, Juan de Escovedo, to Madrid to get help from the King.

Antonio Pérez, Philip's secretary, a man devoured by ambition for power, influenced Philip to believe that Escovedo was responsible for Don John's failure to carry out a peace policy in Flanders and suggested that Escovedo be done away with.

By subtle arguments the wily Pérez clouded Philip's judgment to the point where the monarch agreed that Escovedo was a threat to the good of the kingdom and ought to be removed.

Pérez tried three times unsuccessfully to poison Escovedo and then had the man secretly stabbed by some hired assassins. The murder took place at night in a lonely lane between Escovedo's home and the palace of Ana, the one-eyed Princess of Éboli.

After Ana's abortive attempt to be a nun, she had begun a relationship with Antonio Pérez, who was often seen at her palace. She was later accused of being an accessory to the murder of Escovedo. Her role may have been the revenge of an enraged woman. She had been taken by surprise in some unseemly behavior with Pérez one day when Escovedo made an unexpected visit to her palace. Escovedo, who had been a close friend of Ruy Gómez, Ana's deceased husband, was angry to see his friend's memory disgraced, and he upbraided the widow for scandalous conduct. A guilty woman exposed makes a ruthless enemy. Shortly after this incident Escovedo was murdered.

Not long after the assassination, rumor began to spread, whispered at first but then openly spoken, that Pérez and Ana were involved in the crime. From that day Philip had no peace. His own implication in the foul deed made him hold back the arm of justice. Notwithstanding, Pérez was eventually arrested and imprisoned, but he escaped and fled to France and then to England and back again to France where hc died in exile in 1611, thirteen years after the death of Philip.

Historians tell us that the disgraced man died repentant and shriven. He may have owed his salvation to Teresa's dearly loved nun, Ana de San Bartolomé, who prayed daily in her Carmelite convent for his soul. Pérez's one-eyed accomplice was placed under house arrest until her death in 1592.

The report of Escovedo's murder did not reach Don John until summer although the event took place in March. By then Philip had also sent money and men.

John continued to gain control in the Lowlands, but in September he suddenly took ill and died in camp at Tirlemont outside Namur. Whether he was poisoned or died of the pestilence that was decimating the enemy's ranks has never been satisfactorily determined.

He was buried in the Escorial Philip had built, a monumental palace, monastery, church, mausoleum, all in one. They laid the young man's body next to that of his illustrious father, the Emperor, Charles V. On the marble above his remains were inscribed the words that Pius V was reported miraculously to have heard before appointing Don John Commander-in-Chief of the Lepanto fleet: "There was a man sent from God whose name was John."

34

The Count of Tendilla's temper had scarcely cooled from his encounter with Gracián when his anger flared again. What was this nonsense he was hearing about a restraining Decree to Madre Teresa from Felipe Sega, the Nuncio? Would they never leave that holy woman in peace?

The Count gathered a few grandees from the Court and approached King Philip who, though busy with affairs of the realm, listened to the Count's report. Shortly afterward Philip summoned the Nuncio to Court.

Though there were many lords of the realm and bishops who hastened to tell the Nuncio the truth, all their efforts would have profited but little had not God made use of the King.

"It has come to my attention," the King said to Sega, "that the Calced are fighting the Discalced Carmelite nuns and friars. It is with profound displeasure that I hear of these attacks against people who have always practiced the greatest austerity and perfection. I have further been told that you

180

make no effort to help the Discalced. See to it that in the future you line yourself on the side of virtue."

Sega made no reply. He had his authority from Rome, but he was conscious of the power exercised by this black-clad potentate before him.

Philip appointed a committee to investigate the dispute. The Nuncio was made to sit in on the deliberations. Up until this time Sega's information about the Discalced had been from their enemies. Now he was hearing the other side. He immediately saw how mistaken his judgments had been. To his credit, he at once withdrew his opposition and aligned himself with the monarch in begging recognition from Rome for a free and separate province for the Discalced.

Teresa had the first intimation that all was well again when, in May 1579, she received a letter from Padre Ángel de Salazar, the Carmelite Provincial. "Madre Teresa," he wrote, "continue with your activities and the visitation of your convents."

Teresa needed no second directive. She was sixty-four and not well, but the Provincial's letter renewed her vigor. On June 25, she traveled to Salamanca to settle some legal difficulties over the ownership of the nuns' house. On her way she spent a few days at Medina and Valladolid.

Teresa stayed at Salamanca for more than two months. While there, she received a letter from Doña Luisa de Cerda who was building a new convent for the nuns at Malagón. Teresa wanted to go directly to the place, but on the way she had a heart attack and suffered a stroke of palsy. She stopped at Ávila where she spent several weeks regaining her health. Teresa had never let physical ills interfere with her activities. She felt that the less attention she paid to her aches and pains, the better. But there was a limit to her endurance and more and more her body was giving away.

It was November 25 before she reached Malagón. She was ill again and scarcely able to move about, but she went immediately to the construction site. "This house should be completed by December 8," she told the workmen as she looked over the new structure.

"Impossible, Madre!" said the man in charge. "More likely six months."

But the man had never dealt with Teresa. With only her determination keeping her on her feet, she urged on the workers, supervised their labors, insisted on eating her lunch on the construction site, and had the men work by flares half the night while she stayed with them, encouraging them and goading them on.

On December 8, the nuns moved in and opened the new convent. Some work had still to be done, but the building could be used and the house went into action. The next day Teresa had another attack of palsy.

All Teresa's other convents had been old buildings adapted to cloister living. The new Malagón convent was built with nuns in mind. It was so much to Teresa's liking that she planned to stay a while even after she felt better. She would have gone through with this decision and remained at Malagón except for a summons from Villanueva de la Jara, a small town between Toledo and Valencia.

At Villanueva were nine women who several years earlier had banded together and agreed to live as a community. They had a plan of life and followed it closely without affiliating themselves with any Order. Each of the nine women took her turn as superior or worked in any capacity where a need was felt.

The parish priest at Villanueva had always wanted Teresa to establish these *señoras* as Carmelite nuns. Teresa had hesitated because she felt that the women were too settled in their ways to be able to accept a new mode of living. She also wondered if the town could support a convent dependent on alms. The distance away from her other convents was another consideration. Villanueva lay twenty-eight leagues from the nearest Carmelite house.

Teresa arrived at the village on February 21, 1580, and went immediately to the home of the nine women. They were all there, lined up in the narrow hallway of their small home, waiting to greet her—nine thin, apparently half-starved, shabbily dressed *señoras,* their faces transformed with happiness. Teresa's heart was conquered, and she opened the convent on the same day. She got Carmelite habits for the group as soon as she could and was moved to tears when they told her how long they had prayed for the blessed privilege of wearing the vesture of Our Lady of Mount Carmel.

Padre Antonio, Teresa's first Reform prior, had come with her. He took over teaching the nine new nuns the recitation of the Hours. Since only one of the nine could read, he allowed them a shorter form of prayer, the Little Office of Our Lady.

Teresa had the joy, not long afterward, of hearing that Rome had approved the King's and the Nuncio's appeals for a separate province for the Discalced and that her beloved Gracián had been appointed its first provincial—even if by a majority of but one vote. She took care, however, not to appear too jubilant for the sake of Antonio who had hoped to be appointed to the position.

35

Teresa left Villanueva de la Jara on March 20, 1580 and arrived at Toledo on March 26. Five days later she fell sick with influenza that was sweeping Europe that year. When she left Toledo in the beginning of May, she was still feeling weak, but the weather was beautiful, and by the time she reached Segovia on June 13 her spirits were high and she seemed never to have been ill.

She had scarcely packed her bags for a few days' stopover in Segovia when she received a message that her brother Lorenzo had died. She immediately hurried back to Ávila for his funeral.

Lorenzo's death left a void in Teresa's heart. They had grown so close since his return to Spain, and he was so open to grace, that she had been able to direct him into profound levels of prayer. Now he was gone. The unexpected deaths of Don Francisco de Salcedo and of her former Jesuit confessor, Father Baltasar Álvarez, added to Teresa's sense of loneliness.

After Lorenzo's funeral and the necessary delay to settle family affairs, Teresa went forward toward Palencia. By August 8, she had reached Valladolid, where her niece, María Bautista (María Ocampo), was Prioress.

María was thirty-seven at this time. She was still a beautiful woman and had become an efficient Prioress, but the years had robbed her of some of her religious fervor. On more than one occasion Teresa had found it necessary to reprove María for her quick temper and her independent spirit. At the same time Teresa loved this woman with the deep, possessive affection she kept for all her relatives, and if she sometimes thought wistfully of the fervent young nun who, in unquestioning obedience, once planted a rotten vegetable, Teresa now accepted the brisk, assertive Prioress of Valladolid as she found her.

Teresa was so ill when she came to Valladolid that María Bautista put her to bed immediately and the nuns thought she was going to die. She was up again in a week, but she was changed. For the first time she had begun to show her age and looked like an old woman. But her spirit was as vigorous as ever, and before the end of the year she was feeling well enough to move forward according to her plans. By June 14, 1581 she had founded the convent at Palencia and another at Soria. The same month she returned to Ávila.

She barely set her foot inside the house when the nuns voted to make her Prioress. This small convent, Teresa's first, was no longer as it had been when she founded it. The nuns were unhappy and the discipline was lax. Teresa looked about for the cause. Much of the blame fell on Padre Julián, the old chaplain. He had been here too long, had grown less observant, and had relaxed a number of the rules. When Teresa took over the position of prioress, Julián grumbled at her interference, but he reluctantly cooperated.

The nuns were at fault, too. Teresa reminded them that they had once begged her to write some counsels for their guidance. She had done this, giving them the *Way of Perfection*.

Sitting among them now and speaking in her warm, familiar way, she helped them remember how she had stressed charity, love of God and love of neighbor. And she questioned them. Had they forgotten how she had cautioned them against dangerous friendships, those particular attachments of the heart that lead a nun to single out one other nun to the exclusion of the rest of the Community and bestow on that individual an engrossing affection, destroying God's love in them both?

And what were they doing about helping one another in bearing the burden of everyday living, about rejoicing in each other's spiritual progress, in showing themselves happy to serve one another in the lowliest tasks?

They sat around her, listening, knowing she was right in what she said, resolving in their hearts to be worthy of their Madre who, in her humble holiness, seemed to draw God down into their midst.

Each day she spoke to them brought to their minds what she had written. Had they forgotten that section in the book where she had stressed detachment and mortification?

Some of the younger nuns were unduly preoccupied with the problems of their relatives. Thinking of her own numerous relatives and the difficulties she had seen them experience over the years, Teresa could sympathize with these young nuns. But she showed them how an exaggerated involvement with the problems of relatives was contrary to a true love for them, a love that viewed all happenings in the light of eternity. It was all in the book she had written. Let them read it again.

To the older nuns who complained that they were not advancing in prayer, Teresa suggested that they read once more her admonition on silence and solitude. The voice of the Beloved is the faintest of whispers. How could they hope to hear it if they were not silent and alone in their cells?

Teresa's greatest concern was that the nuns be humble. "Sisters," she assured them, "it is the humble nun who lives in the truth. Humility is a greater gift than favors in prayer."

And why were they afraid to be corrected for their faults when such corrections furthered their spiritual growth?

Teresa spoke and acted gently, leading them by kindness. But when one day she encountered a few nuns who were strong on asserting their "rights"—they were older, they had been in the Community longer, and (God forbid!) they had come from titled families—Teresa was convinced that the spirit of evil had entered the house, and she was vehement in her denunciation. Rights? One can see her black eyes flashing. The only rights a true follower of Jesus should claim was the right to be formed into the likeness of the Crucified Lord. "Sisters," she told them, "if you can't bring yourselves to live in the spirit of our Holy Rule, which is one of humility, you would do better to leave."

Teresa had been in Ávila about five months when John of the Cross visited her on November 28. They had not seen each other for a year and Teresa welcomed him warmly. Each time she saw this holy friar, her admiration for him increased. Gracián was still first in her affections—and would always be—but she realized more and more that the course of the Reform would have been less tumultuous had it proceeded under the stabilizing influence of this unpretentious friar who burned with white-hot love for God.

John was almost boyishly happy to see Teresa again. Furthermore, he had come with a purpose, a happy suggestion, and he anticipated her pleasure.

"Madre," he said after they had exchanged a few casual remarks. "I've brought a carriage and mules to take you and some nuns with me to open a new convent at Granada."

Even before he finished, he saw from Teresa's face that she had other plans.

"I'm sorry, Padre. I can't do it. I've already promised to found a convent at Burgos."

John had looked forward to this trip to Ávila and the return with Madre Teresa to Granada. Thinking of it beforehand had been one of the rare human joys he had allowed himself. Now it had come to naught.

187

He did not stay long at Ávila. When he returned to Granada, Teresa sent along two nuns to open the convent. The trip back was long for John. For all his nearness to God he loved this woman who had figured so prominently in the direction of his life, and the failure of his plan to take her with him was a sharp disappointment.

Did he know that Gracián would accompany Teresa to Burgos? Was the holy friar still capable of a little natural envy? If so, the shadow of its passing over his soul served only to make him reassess his spirit of detachment, to call back to his mind the need to sever any ties that still bound him to the things of earth. When he arrived home, John took out Teresa's letters that he had saved over the years and, building a little fire in the monastery garden, dropped them one by one into the flames, destroying the only human treasure to which his heart still clung.

Teresa felt John's disappointment. She wished that circumstances could have been different and that she could have gone with him to Granada. But she had no time to brood over her feelings. Burgos was ahead of her. She commended their mutual hurt to God, and on January 2 she left Ávila accompanied by Gracián, who had just returned from Salamanca, Sister Ana de San Bartolomé, who watched over Teresa more than ever now with all her illnesses, and six other nuns.

The weather was cold. It snowed or rained all the way. The group passed through Medina, then went to Valladolid where they spent a few days with María Bautista and continued on. The roads were washed out in many places, and accommodations at the inns were poor.

At one point where the danger was great in crossing a river, Teresa insisted on going ahead in a carriage to see how safe it would be. "If I fall into the river and drown, all of you go back to the inn and wait for better weather."

Teresa did not drown, but the carriage had scarcely rolled into the river when it upset. Teresa jumped out into the cold current that came almost up to her knees. "Lord," she cried, holding her skirts and shivering in the icy water, "we've put up with so much already, and now this."

The Voice she had learned to love came back: "Teresa, this is the way I treat My friends."

The Divine irony was not lost on Teresa. "Then, Lord," she replied, her wry humor coming from between chattering teeth, "it's understandable that You have so few." It was the familiar exchange between two hearts at home in each other's love. Teresa had already been granted the intimacy of the Spiritual Marriage, but in her everyday life it was consummated in suffering and the way of the Cross.

They reached Burgos on January 26. They were dirty, wet, and cold. Doña Catalina de Tolosa, a friend, offered Teresa and her nuns some rooms in her home until they could find other lodgings. She seated them around her huge hearth and dried them out as best she could. The next day Teresa was desperately ill.

I was suffering from a troublesome sore throat which I had contracted on the road to Valladolid; I still had a temperature and eating caused me the greatest pain.

However, she sent word to the Archbishop of Burgos to let him know they had arrived.

The prelate bristled when he got Teresa's message. *They? Who were they?* His Excellency had not asked her to bring nuns. He had agreed to talk with *her*. Let her take her nuns home.

Teresa realized that there had been a misunderstanding, but taking her nuns back was the last thing she intended to do. As soon as she felt well enough to be on her feet, she rented two attic rooms above a hospital while she looked about town for a house.

The oak and beech forests around the city of Burgos

189

were beginning to bud before Teresa got the Archbishop's approval. She opened the new convent on April 19.

I am still suffering from this sore throat, though it is the end of June . . . it is . . . extremely painful.

On July 26 Teresa and Ana de San Bartolomé finally left Burgos for Ávila. They planned to stop once more at Valladolid. There had been some family squabbling over a bequest that Lorenzo had left for the chapel at St. Joseph's in Ávila, and Teresa wanted to talk over the matter with María Bautista at Valladolid.

To Teresa's surprise, María took sides against her and grew violently angry. When Teresa realized that it was impossible to come to some agreement with María, she gathered her bags and left the convent immediately. María walked Teresa and Ana de San Bartolomé to the door. "Get out of here, both of you," she snapped. "Don't ever show your face here again."

It is a quirk of fate that this unguarded outburst should live on for more than four hundred years to throw a shadow over the name of an otherwise admirable woman. As for Teresa, one can only guess her feelings as the door slammed behind her. She was certainly unprepared for María's reaction. At the same time María's conduct could not have been totally unexpected. She was a woman at the height of her powers, intelligent, shrewd, thrifty, but a bit more cocksure of herself than in keeping with humility. Over the years Teresa had taken her to task more than once for acting too independently. But Teresa was now a wrinkled old lady, almost physically helpless without the supportive arm of the faithful Ana. Apparently Teresa had insisted that something should be done, and momentarily María's nerves were set on edge. Nevertheless, it is unfortunate that history caught the voice of this really worthy woman at her weakest moment and then failed to record for us the apology or the sorrow that surely must have followed later.

36

Teresa had written ahead to St. Joseph's that she would be in Avila by September 1. She would have kept to this schedule had not Fray Antonio, now vicar of the Discalced province, met her at Medina where Teresa stopped on her way to Ávila, and ordered her to Alba de Tormes.

Teresa was physically in no condition to take on this added burden. The sore throat that had bothered her for eight months had developed into a raw ulcer and ruptured to the outside, her heart was bad, the arm she had broken five years earlier was as useless as ever, and she walked only with difficulty.

Antonio was blind to all this. He had become so accustomed to the force of Teresa's indomitable spirit that he failed to notice when her body was no longer able to follow.

The Medina Prioress remonstrated. "Why the hurry, Padre?"

"Emergency," he replied. The Duchess of Alba, Doña María Enríquez, a friend of the Reform, was calling for Teresa to pray over her daughter-in-law who was about to give birth to a child.

Teresa would not allow herself to complain, though she

later admitted to Ana de San Bartolomé that she had never found a superior's command more difficult to accept. She got into the coach the Duchess had sent, and two days later arrived in Alba de Tormes on the eve of St. Matthew. By then she was too sick to see the Duchess' daughter-in-law. Nor was it necessary since the baby had arrived and all was well.

The Prioress at Alba de Tormes, Juana del Espíritu Santo, was alarmed at Teresa's appearance. "Madre, go to bed immediately." She led Teresa to her room, and Ana de San Bartolomé helped the sick woman undress. As Teresa stretched herself under the covers of the narrow cot, she turned to Ana. "In twenty years I haven't gone to bed so early, but God knows I need to. I've never been so tired."

She had reasons to be tired. For a score of years she had traveled throughout Spain, on muleback, in wagons, coaches, carts, on foot. She had weathered the raw winds that sweep down the sides of the Sierras and blow across the treeless plains. At times she had pushed forward on roads where the mud was so deep it churned about the axle hubs of her cart. Unable to bear heat, she had journeyed hundreds of leagues in canvas-topped wagons under a torrid sun.

She was tired, too, of arguing with bishops, bargaining with merchants, goading on workmen; tired of looking for houses, settling family disputes, being at the beck and call of "fine ladies."

Teresa was also tired of writing. In obedience to her confessors she had written her autobiography and a lengthy account of the founding of each new convent. She had also written the *Way of Perfection,* a book of principles to guide her spiritual daughters in their practice of virtue, and *The Interior Castle and Mansions,* her treatise on the progressive steps to intimacy with God in prayer. There were other writings, too, and hundreds of letters.

None of this writing had been done leisurely. Teresa had to snatch moments here and there from her busy days. Often, after the nuns were in bed for the night, she sat in her cell, writing by the light of a candle, while the cold winds blew past the canvas covering that served as a window and chilled her fingers until she had to rub them together to be able to continue writing.

Now she turned on her pallet and slept. The next morning, September 21, she felt well enough to get up and attend Mass. For about a week she seemed somewhat better. On the feast of St. Michael, however, she had a severe hemorrhage. Three days later, October 2, she was unable to rise. She told Ana de San Bartolomé that she was going to die soon, and she asked for a confessor.

Padre Antonio came to the sickroom. The elderly Prior knelt by Teresa's bed and heard her confession of faults so trivial that there was little matter for absolution. Afterward he sat by her bed and spoke with her. He seemed contrite for having pushed her beyond her endurance. "Madre, beg Our Lord to let you live a little longer."

Teresa regarded him quietly. Did her mind go back fifteen years to her first impressions of this man? He had never quite measured up to her expectations. Yet she must have realized that she was always comparing him with John of the Cross and later with Gracián, both of whom she placed far out ahead of all other men. Teresa would not live to know that Antonio was to remain faithful to the austere practices of the Primitive Rule until he died, an old man in his nineties. She looked at him now and smiled. "Padre, my work is done. Why should I stay on?"

Antonio left the room to get the Blessed Sacrament. When he returned with the Holy Viaticum, Teresa raised herself from the low pallet. She was trembling with weakness, but her worn-out body caught fire from her soul. She fixed her eyes on the Sacred Host with tears of joy. "Jesus, my Bridegroom! At last the hour has come. I will go to see You face to face forever." She had hoped that this Communion would be the end. Instead, she gained physical strength from the Eucharist.

Toward evening she asked to be anointed. Padre Antonio came with the Holy Oils. Afterward Teresa spoke to the nuns gathered about her bedside. "My daughters, I beg you that when I am gone, you will continue to observe the Rule." Then she asked their pardon. "Sisters, if ever I have hurt any of you or given a bad example, forgive me."

The nuns wept.

Teresa suffered intense pain during the night, but her soul remained rapt in ecstasy.

All the next day she lay quiet, absorbed in prayer. From time to time, Ana de San Bartolomé, who never left her side, heard her whisper, "I am a daughter of the Church." And sometimes, "A contrite and humbled heart, O God, You will not despise."

Toward evening her condition grew worse. Padre Antonio came to the sickroom, and the nuns stood about with lighted candles, praying softly. Teresa lay with her eyes closed, her face calm and radiant. A little before nine o'clock she suddenly opened her eyes and gazed about. She seemed perplexed, as if she were looking for someone and could not find her. Immediately one of the nuns went for Ana de San Bartolomé who, at Antonio's insistence, had left the room to get something to eat while the other nuns kept vigil at Teresa's bedside.

As soon as Ana came into the room, Teresa relaxed and closed her eyes. Her whole appearance became transformed. The wrinkles of age disappeared, and her face took on a youthful beauty.

Ana knelt and slipped her arm under the dying woman's shoulders, lifting her slightly to ease her breathing. Teresa's eyelids fluttered and she gave a faint moan. Then she was quiet again while the light of the candles flickered on her face and there was only the soft sound of the nuns praying the *Credo*.

A little while after, Teresa drew in a short, quick breath, sighed gently, and expired, dying as much "from love" as from her many illnesses. Her head fell to the side and rested against the strong shoulder of the faithful Ana.

Teresa of Ahumada was dead. The woman, who as a child of six set out to find heaven, had come to the end of her long journey. God. Eternity. At last.

It was nine o'clock on the evening of October 4, 1582.

Epilogue

The day after her death Teresa was buried in a grave near the Alba convent where she had died. Nine months later, when the nuns at Ávila begged that her remains be brought to St. Joseph's, Gracián and those who helped exhume and transfer Teresa's unembalmed body found it incorrupt. It remains that way today.

On April 24, 1614, thirty-two years after her death, the same year that her beloved Gracián died, Pope Paul V beatified Teresa. Eight years later, 1622, Gregory XV canonized this great Spanish woman.

As early as 1588, when her manuscripts were first published through the efforts of Luis de León, a writer of the period, Teresa's name became immortal. Since then millions have read her books and been inspired by their heavenly doctrine. It was in recognition of the contribution that Teresa's writings have made to the spiritual treasury of the Church that Pope Paul VI, on September 27, 1970, proclaimed Teresa a Doctor of the Church, an honor held by only one other woman, Saint Catherine of Siena.

Teresa's writings are not all that have kept her name alive. Today she lives on in the more than 3,000 Discalced Carmelite men and close to 15,000 Carmelite nuns scattered in Reform monasteries throughout the world.

* * *

The Universal Church celebrates the feast of St. Teresa of Ávila on October 15. The Communion verse of the Mass for the day is from Psalm 88 and echoes Teresa's constant song of praise: "Forever will I sing the goodness of the Lord."

197

Sources Consulted

The Dust of Her Sandals by A. De Castro Albarran (translated by Sister Mary Bernarda, B.V.M.)

Teresa of Ávila by Marcelle Auclair

St. Teresa of Avila by John Beevers

The letters of St. Teresa (translated and annotated by the Benedictines of Stanbrook, Vols. 1 and 2)

The Story of Don John of Austria by Luis Coloma, S.J. (translated by Lady Moreton)

Selected Writings of St. Teresa of Avila by William J. Doheny

The Council of Trent by James A. Froude

Peregrinaciones de Anastasio by Jerónimo Gracián

Saint Teresa by Elizabeth Hamilton

Santa Teresa de Avila by Helmut A. Hatzfeld

Erasmus and the Age of Reformation by Johan Huizinga

A History of the Council of Trent by Hubert Jedin (translated by Dom Ernest Graf, O.S.B., Vol. 1)

Saint Teresa by Henri Joly (translated by Emily Waller)

The Collected Works of St. Teresa of Avila (translated by Kieran Kavanaugh, O.C.D., and Otilio Rodriguez, O.C.D., Vols. 1 and 2)

Meet Saint Teresa by Joseph P. Kelly

Life of St. John of the Cross by David Lewis

A History of Spain by Harold Livermore

Teresa de Jesús by Walker Lowry

The Life of St. Peter of Alcántara by Francesco Marchese

A History of Iberian Civilization by Oliveira Martins (translated by Aubrey F. G. Bell)

Heirs of St. Teresa of Avila by Winifred Nevin

Teresa of Avila, the Woman by Winifred Nevin

For One Sweet Grape by Kate O'Brien

Teresa of Avila by Kate O'Brien

Complete Works of St. Theresa (translated and edited by E. Allison Peers from the critical edition of P. Silverio de Santa Teresa, O.C.D., Vols. I–III)

Handbook to the Life and Times of St. Teresa and St. John of the Cross by E. Allison Peers

Mother of Carmel by E. Allison Peers

The Story of the Carmelite Order by Peter-Thomas Rohrback, O.C.D.

Vida de Teresa de Ávila (Vols. I–V) by P. Silverio de Santa Teresa, O.C.D.

Carmelite and Poet by Robert Sencourt (Robert Esmonde Gordon George)

Saint Teresa of Ávila by William T. Walsh